John Macksoud's *Other Illusions*

Philosophy/Communication
Ramsey Eric Ramsey, Series Editor

John Macksoud's *Other Illusions: Inquiries Toward a Rhetorical Theory*

By Craig R. Smith

Purdue University Press
West Lafayette, Indiana

Printed in the United States of America.

Library of Congress Cataloging-in-Publication Data

Macksoud, John, 1934-2005.
  [Other illusions]
  John Macksoud's Other illusions / [introduction and
commentary by] Craig R. Smith.
      p. cm. -- (Philosophy/communication series)
   ISBN 978-1-55753-515-3
  1. Rhetoric--Philosophy. I. Smith, Craig R. II. Title.
   PN175.M115 2008
   808'.001--dc22
                              2009007087

Contents

Introduction to and Commentary on John Macksoud's *Other Illusions: Inquiries Toward a Rhetorical Theory*

In January of 2005, John Macksoud was found dead in his remote home in the Pennsylvania woods. His will left all of his possessions and works to me. I had been a student of John's in the mid-1960s and remained a friend and collaborator for the rest of his life. After putting his papers in order and a few months of grieving, I decided that the most fitting tribute to him would be to publish posthumously his previously unpublished works. *Other Illusions* is the most important of these works, of which only a few printed copies remain. I have scanned my copy into a PDF file so that its form is retained by the publisher; the way certain sentences fall on the page is important to their interpretation.

This introduction proceeds in two stages. First, it reviews Macksoud's academic career to put the work in context. Second, it summarizes and comments on *Other Illusions*.

Academic Career

John Macksoud saw the world in a revolutionary, some would say subversive, way. As early as 1964, he began to resurrect the Sophists and to move toward a post-structural approach to language use. He was ahead of his time but few noticed. As readers shall see, though Macksoud won several awards from the Speech Communication Association for scholarly articles, his book on post-structuralism was not embraced by the field because the book broke with traditional academic form. It is interesting to note that in 1966, at a conference at Johns Hopkins University, scholarly papers were presented that attacked the structuralism of Levy-Strauss but did not receive widespread notice for several years. The conference was attended by such future lights as Michel Foucault, Paul DeMan, and Jacques Derrida. In the 1970s, this work bubbled its way to Yale University's English Department, which then invited Derrida to visit. Deconstructionism was launched amid much controversy and hoopla across America.

At the same time, Macksoud was trying to get his book published, but publishers insisted on changes that Macksoud refused to complete. He was making a gesture as a lone voice in the sub-field of rhetoric in departments of speech communication. At the time, that field was caught in a vicious civil war between quantitative studies of "communication theory" and traditional humanistic studies of "rhetorical theory." Macksoud not only attacked the methodology of the social scientists, he broke with the rigorous and heavily footnoted approach of the humanists. Macksoud's playful gesture was ignored by the social scientists and suppressed by the humanists. When Macksoud took the book to those he knew in English departments, notably Ralph Cohen then at UCLA, he was told his work was too radical and subversive to be published. Macksoud then decided to publish the book himself in Santa Barbara in 1973. He distributed it to many thinkers and opinion leaders, but no one responded. Thus, credit for the birth of deconstructionism and post-structural thought went to others who revolted from Levi-Strauss but did so in traditional academic form.

John Macksoud was born in 1934 in Brooklyn, the son of Lebanese Catholic immigrants, who moved to Los Angeles after World War II. He was educated in Catholic schools including Loyola High School where he learned the art of argumentation from the Jesuits. After a stint at a junior college or two, he entered UCLA where he honed his skills on the debate team. After he finished his Bachelor of Arts in 1957 in psychology, he entered UCLA Law School but stayed only one year, deciding to pursue a Ph.D. in speech communication instead. He completed a dissertation on the interpretive theory of Kenneth Burke in 1964. In the fall of that year, he became an assistant professor at the University of California at Santa Barbara.

At the invitation of the University, Kenneth Burke had become that year's Regents' Lecturer. From late October to early December, he delivered four public lectures and taught a seminar, which he allowed me to audit, even though I was an undergraduate. Burke's lectures were converted into *Language As Symbolic Action*—subsequently published in 1966. Macksoud's dissertation entitled "The Literary Theories of Kenneth Burke and the Discovery of Meanings in Oral Interpretation" provided his entrée to Burke, and the two became fast friends, as did their wives.

In the early 1970s, while he worked on his post-structural opus, Macksoud won the Speech Communication Association's Golden Anniversary Award for his analysis of e. e. cummings' "Anyone's How Town." Macksoud's treatment appeared in *Speech Monographs*, edited by Professor Carroll Arnold. He won another major award for his study of Ludwig Wittengenstein. Macksoud wrote two articles on Burkean theory, one for the *Western Journal of Speech Communication* and one for the *Quarterly Journal of Speech*. Macksoud also appeared with some regularity on Speech Communication Association (SCA) and Western Speech Communication Assocation (WSCA) panels on oral interpretation and Burkean studies. For example, at the 1974 SCA convention he presented a paper called "Diotima, Where is Thy Sting?" on a panel entitled "Burkean Dialectic: A Symposium on the Philosophy of Rhetoric."

In 1973, however, Macksoud broke with tradition by self-publishing *Other Illusions: Inquiries Toward a Rhetorical Theory*, in which he wrote, "My debt to Kenneth Burke in print and in person is substantial." Despite my two favorable reviews, first in *Philosophy and Rhetoric* and then in the *Quarterly Journal of Speech*,[1] the book did not have a significant impact on the field, nor was it often cited. In one review I remarked that "because the book is so very well written, even if a little cryptic, because it is so cogent, so tightly reasoned, so charmingly persuasive, it is the most subversive work on rhetoric since the Gorgias." The book advances relativism with at least three major claims: 1) descriptions are always partial because they can never cover all of the things that touch on the web the subject creates; hence, descriptions are edited, that is, they are subject to rhetorical choice; 2) utterances cannot be repeated without a difference in terms of delivery, time, place, style, and/or myriad other rhetorical conditions; and 3) texts can never be read *out* of context, only in *another* context. Though he did not know it at the time, Macksoud was on the cutting edge of what would become post-structural thought. Unfortunately for Macksoud, the theory was attributed to DeMan, Foucault, and particularly Derrida because of his *Of Grammatology*. Although *Of Grammatology* was published in France in 1967, it was not made available in English translation until 1974, a year after Macksoud's self-publication. Hence, Macksoud was not aware of Derrida's work when writing *Other Illusions*; he composed a new theory on language independent of Derrida that paralleled the Frenchman's work. However, Macksoud's work went unrecognized because of its playful break with tradition and the fact that it was overshadowed by the leonine reputation of Derrida. Macksoud was a rhetorician grappling with these issues a decade before anyone else his field; however, he was also a voice crying in the wilderness because of the insecurities of that field at the time. Macksould was denied tenure at UC Santa Barbara, but he received a one year extension on his contract due to litigation. The school's administration then refused to recognize *Other Illusions* as a scholarly work, and he was ultimately denied tenure again in 1973.

In that year, Macksoud moved to the English Department at the State University of New York at Binghamton where he published his last scholarly pieces. In 1977, he refused to be considered for tenure, because he now believed it to be immoral. He believed tenure contributed to a two-class society. In sympathy, I resigned my tenure at the University of Alabama in Birmingham (UAB) and insisted on being evaluated in the same manner as the assistant professors. While UAB cooperated with my request—I was a full professor and a department chair—SUNY Binghamton did not allow John the same privilege, fearing a sanction from the American Association of University Professors (AAUP). He resigned his position.

In the winter of 1979, I took a quarter-long leave of absence from UAB to teach at Northwestern University. I gave my classes at UAB to John. They were the last he taught. After the quarter ended, he returned to Binghamton and took up with one of his former students, Judy Genkin. By this time, John's wife, to whom *Other Illusions* is dedicated, had divorced him and taken their child Meredith back to California. John moved into a home we jointly constructed and owned in rural Madera, Pennsylvania. John had an enormous musical talent and had written a number of ballads, putting words to them. I reconfigured these ballads into three musicals that languish on my shelf. By 1983, I was living in Washington, D.C., as President of the Freedom of Expression Foundation, so it was not difficult for me to drive and visit with John, which I did regularly. He had become almost completely reclusive. Judy, who lived nearby, visited him daily. He and I spoke on the phone often, but in 1986, he informed me that he no longer wanted me to visit the house: "Bodies get in the way," he told me. He wanted our conversations to continue by phone only.

When his heart began to fail him, he allowed Judy to move into the house to care for him. I continued to speak with him via phone every week. In January of 2005, Judy came home from errands and found John had died. She then committed suicide.

While his former students work on other projects, I have taken it upon myself to publish *Other Illusions*, his most important work. It is followed by an essay by Greg Desilet, a former student of John's, who compares his work with that of Derrida in very detailed and revealing way.

Other Illusions

On the surface, the admonitions and playful nature of the book explain why Macksoud became controversial and perhaps why he was not granted tenure at UC Santa Barbara. More important, the book reinforces a strain of relativistic theory that retrieves the Sophists[2] and extends through Jacques Derrida to the present where many of us deal with constructed realities in our rhetorical theories. Macksoud was also offering a warning about pseudo-scientific research, a Philippic against the quantitative approach in the field. He not only attempted to reveal the rhetorical nature of their use of the scientific method, he tried to show that science itself was at base rhetorical. Those in communication theory who have backed into "qualitative" methods may find that Macksoud was decades ahead of them. In short, Macksoud's 1973 publication presaged major postmodern thinking, and if it had received proper attention, the book may have shaped that thinking in substantial ways.

Macksoud sees the world in a different way, and that view may prove important to current scholarship. However, it cannot accomplish this unless readers become as playful as Macksoud about the rigors and fetters of academic form. That is because the book threatened the established order of the academic community. The book was self-published by the author, not by a university press or a textbook publisher. In conversations with me, Macksoud claimed that editors and publishers sought revisions that ruined the spirit of the book in attempts to make it conform to academic standards. He insisted on retaining control of the publishing process, and the only way he could do that was to take it to a local printer in Santa Barbara.

Furthermore, the book, reproduced from scanning for this volume, is only ninety-five pages long, a monograph really, and some of the pages contain only three or four lines. The book has no footnotes. It makes passing reference to common statements in Plato, Aristotle, and Shakespeare without citing chapter and verse. It cites no contemporary scholarly works, but in several places the text relies on dialogue from films, again without attribution. For these egregious practices, it was once criticized by two tenure and promotion committees. Some read Macksoud's method to mean that he had little respect for the academic community; others argued that Macksoud was seeking a larger audience. He refused to comment on these attributed motives but did admit that he sought to stir up debate of scholarly expectations.

The book uses anecdotes, sayings, stories, and even jokes to mark off sections and to initiate new lines of thought. These devices were deemed subversive rather than performative, because they are rarely, if ever, used in academic prose, and because the messages they carry undercut normal ways of thinking. However, it is his wit and Zeno-like argumentative skills that are used to craft these episodes into representations of the limits and relativity of language. Pages fifty-nine through sixty-four contain only nine lines. They constitute a riddle that begins a new section of the book. The riddle goes like this:

What is it that is orange, hangs from the ceiling, and whistles?

I don't know.

A horse.

Why is it orange?

Because I painted it orange.

Why does it hang from the ceiling?

Because I hung it there.

Why does it whistle?

I don't know.

These forms are rare in academic writing. They seem inspired more by Lewis Carroll than by Kenneth Burke, a man who was not afraid to break the bounds of academia when given the chance. Burke never finished his bachelor's degree, let alone a Ph.D. Conversely, Macksoud had already won two awards for his scholarship, proving he had mastered the standard form. His humerous and layered approach was a new tactic.

More important to my point, however, are the ways in which the book provides a corrective to the substance of what we do and write in the academic world. The first third of the book attempts to undercut the grounds for quantitative research, particularly in the social sciences. It may explain why, quite sensibly, the courts have regularly rejected such research as admissible evidence in law cases. Macksoud was particularly appalled at those who relied on B. F. Skinner to justify their methods. At one point Macksoud writes, "I want to show you that the stimulus-response pattern is inescapably causal…and that it will not tolerate reduction from connection to correlation." He later argues that "probability and frequency are the children of *elegance*." Because no social scientist can ever account for all variables, Macksoud argues that social science is clearly rhetorical and interpretive. He concludes, "Perhaps we should value science not, as we are inclined to do, because it can do so much, but rather because it can do the little it does so well."

Macksoud admonishes readers not to rely on social scientific theories based on quantitative research because the case they make is neither causal nor correlational. These social scientific inventions are rhetorical since they must rationalize why variables are relevant or irrelevant. Furthermore, his critique precedes much of the work now underway on the rhetoric of science, which extends this line of thinking, and the move from quantitative to qualitative analysis on the social scientific side of the discipline.

Macksoud's attack on "A Scientific Attitude" begins with a quotation from a film (*The Red Shoes*, a favorite of Macksoud's, because he identified with the impresario played by Anton Walbrook) that asserts that a magician cannot pull a rabbit from a hat unless there is a rabbit already in the hat. This is immediately followed by the parable of the magician who raises a corpse from the dead without knowing how he performed the act. Initially, I believed this parable intended to assert that all definitions are relative. In other words, what is the proper definition of "magician"? Does he have to know what he is doing to be a magician? What would make a person into a magician? However, Macksoud claimed that the question to be raised is how do audience members know that someone is a magician? That is, the parable is epistemological; how do we know what we know? By performance? By orthodoxy? By deduction?

The confusion over which question is raised may be a result of the next few paragraphs that deal not with these questions directly, but with the question of how we know what we communicate. Communicating implies sharing, which implies the need for language; that is how we share. Language must refer to percepts—not precepts—and a way to couple them with our sensations. What does "couple with" mean here? Macksoud writes that the "correlation of language and experience should be reliable," which reminds us of Bertrand Russell's theory of correspondence. We correlate perceived phenomena with linguistic reports of others.

Thus, what gets shared is perception, and perception, as Macksoud shows, is neither purely objective nor purely descriptive. The structural approach to these phenomena argues that language outlines phenomena into sense or demonstrates relationships that make sense; that is how we share concepts. However, this theory provides no proof, according to Macksoud, that we really do share. He then moves to the question of why we should test whether we share, noting that a sincere effort here will require an "assumed lack of faith."

What tests will be appropriate for our proof? Russell's "correspondence" won't work because it *already* implies standards for what counts as similarities and differences. Without such standards, the same language could be referring to different phenomena. How do we eliminate the possibility of perceptual equivocation? First, we must admit that the stimulus-response model is in place in all testing. Testing is behavioral, but can it include covert responses? No, since such an inclusion would ruin the paradigm by including communication with rocks and the like. Thus, overt response has to be the index of communicative sharing.

Second, the stimulus-response model is causal and is not reducible to correlation. A response clearly implies a connection, not a correlation. That is, a response is a result of stimuli; it is an effect, not just a simultaneous, uncaused event. So much for David Hume.

Third, certain assumptions are *a priori.* For example, stimuli can recur. If they cannot recur, then we eliminate the possibility of testing and replication, a key to scientific understanding. Another assumption is that there are no internal operative stimuli—otherwise there would be no control over the experiment. This assumption leads to the problem of isolating the operative stimuli in communication situations. On a further note, alleged prediction of a communicative event is actually a prediction that what happened in the past will happen again. For example, a speaker held in high esteem will be more persuasive than a speaker held in low esteem. Thus, we operate in science using an analogical metaphysic that recalls the past, and that helps us to determine the relevant correlations to look for in each case in the future. Kennedy was more persuasive than Nixon because he was held in higher esteem than Nixon. However, note how this "verified" prediction eliminates many other variables that could explain the caused actual outcome. Kennedy was better looking, had a better vocabulary, and had better breeding, among other favorable characteristics.

Look at the problem from a personal perspective. When a command you give is obeyed, your assumption that communication stimulated the response is metaphysically grounded in three ways, all of which either lie outside the realm of controlled variables or require that you fill in some knowledge. Since there is always some variable that is unaccounted for, you must *assume* (on faith?) at some point that you have controlled for the *relevant* variables. Doesn't this reduce our model to one of persuasiveness? We have to persuade ourselves and others of the justification of our grounding and of our selection of variables.

However, the inexhaustible supply of alternative hypotheses, and hence variables, undercuts the method of concomitant variations. Kennedy was more persuasive because he spoke before a Democratic audience; Kennedy was more persuasive because he wore a blue suit; Kennedy was more persuasive because the moon was full. Furthermore, the elimination of one variable may bring another into play. Neither speaker used a microphone, so that is not a relevant variable; however, by not using a microphone, Kennedy had an advantage, because his voice carries farther than Nixon's. Thus, Kennedy's voice may have been more important to his persuasion than his credibility.

Generalizing about recurring variables is also troublesome because each stimulus-response is a single case. To argue that "recurring variables" are relevant is to *generalize* in an unwarranted manner. To put it another way, we must not let scientific simplicity mask aesthetic simplicity. That is the argument from elegance first developed by William of Ockham. The argument that the reduction of variables is convenient is undercut because reducing variables in order to generalize more easily is fraudulent. Macksoud's admonition is important because it has practical implications. In many criminal cases, the simplest explanation is accepted because it conforms to Ockham's razor and saves resources. The most obvious crime suspects are prosecuted for the same reason. In medical situations, the simplest explanation of symptoms is embraced over the more complicated one, which is why people often seek second opinions and why so many diagnoses are incorrect.

These arguments are not trivial to the field of communication because they go to the heart of the question of whether we can talk about communication in any objective way at all, and perhaps we cannot, because it is not causal in the manner of the stimulus-response model. What if we can only talk about communication subjectively? High heat causes water to boil. However, one cannot make similar statements about social scientific analysis of communication situations because they do not lend themselves to the simplicity necessary for scientific causality.

Furthermore, with regard to variables, we cannot know where the path we did not take would have led us. This question can be traced back to David Hume's skepticism. Arguing against the logic of even the simplest scientific claims, Hume might ask: Would the water have boiled at that moment had I not put a flame under it? I cannot know for sure that boiling simply occurs simultaneous with lighting the flame. Thus, that hypothesis can no longer be tested in terms of causality, only in terms of correlations. (Every time I light the flame the water eventually boils.) Once that small leap is made, our faith in testing is based on the *determination* to generalize. We are motivated to make sense of the world, and like Cicero, we are forced to say skepticism is nice in a theoretical discussion or parlor conversation, but you can't run your life that way. You have to accept the cause and effect (intuitively) and move on. However, this need to move on by no means validates our causal assumptions.

Macksoud next moves to the question of probability, which he claims gives more elegance to social scientific research because it is numbers-based. Probability is a rough measure—sometimes made more sharp using numbers, a rhetorical device—of the appearance of constancy of a sequence of events. However, before probability is assessed, the phenomena to be measured must be selected. If I choose to measure the credibility of the speaker, I am choosing a term that has been invented by others and tested by others before me, while excluding, for example, the investigation of pathos. The selection is fouled by the practice of defining it by past experience. Thus, the selection is analogical and self-validating. To put it another way, probabilities are based on the frequencies we select.

Probability is attractive because it is elegant. Think of the scientific column as beginning with causality that is built from probability that relies on frequency, which is an expression of elegance. Elegance results from our desire to select the simplest explanation; we look for common factors, not unique ones, which vary in multiple ways and make things very messy. This love for elegance flows from Ockham and *seems* rational in the modern world that Locke, Kant, and Hegel constructed. Enlightenment—to use Kant's rhetorically loaded term—thinkers and their *deus ex machina* (or intelligent design) followers see a very ordered world. Macksoud, relying on the Sophists, Kierkegaard, and Kenneth Burke, saw a world that was, at best, dramatistic and, at worst, chaotic. Like Derrida, Macksoud did not see order in the world or in language but only relative and contingent meanings, if that. So, he attacked the Enlightenment themes he found in social scientific research.

He began by undermining some of the basic assumptions in science, such as Ockham's razor. First, he claimed that the simplest explanation is selected because it is the simplest to explain. But many of these, such as survival of the fittest, are tautological. That which survives is, by definition, the fittest. Thus, everything that exists is proof of the theory; it has no deniability. For example, one could argue that the Cardinal refutes Darwin's theory because it is red and therefore easy to see and kill. It nests in low shrubs making it vulnerable to cats. But Darwinists reply that the male Cardinal's redness attracts females and nesting in low shrubs prevents Crows from eating its eggs. When the Platypus was discovered, it fit in no genus or phylum of biology, so biologists simply invented a new genus and phylum for the egg bearing mammal.

Second, the simplest explanation is selected because it allows us to generalize without testing every incidence. That is the point of the scientific method. I no longer have to test whether water boils when put over high heat. It is going to happen every time. There are rules in simple science. However, when social scientists seek to emulate these methods, the rules they deduce are not rules at all because they do not produce the same results each time.

What does this say about induction? And does it produce an alternate metaphysic that we incorrectly call empiricism? Elegance controls the scientific community with brute force; it controls interpretation of data and the sorts of models that are acceptable. (We start from *a* theory, *a* principle, *a* hypothesis, not *multiple* ones.) Our object is reduction and simplicity in selecting a hypothesis and then testing that hypothesis. Here we obtain the answer to the opening riddle; elegance enables generalization, and generalization justifies elegance. Generalization is both the child (product) and the father (motive) of elegance. Not even the best magician can pull a rabbit out of a hat unless there is a rabbit already in the hat.

We also generalize to set limits. These limits include the analogous and exclude the dys-analogous. That gives them control and the apparent ability to predict. Analogy thus precedes further generalization. Is this observation? Empiricism? Or is it the past predicting (controlling) the future?

Thus, when we say the scientific method is sound or works, we mean that it is elegant. It explains; it predicts; it allows control; it makes sense of the chaos in the simplest way. However, we have seen that this method is based on analogical generalization, not on absolutely impartial observation. In terms of research into communication phenomenon, we can't achieve the scientific model, even with its flaws, because we are examining phenomenon that are not as simple as boiling water.

Take the question, what does it mean to "know" something? We return to the magician, but this time, instead of pulling a rabbit from the hat, Macksoud has the magician bring a corpse back to life by tapping it. You ask the magician how he does it, and he says, "I'm not sure." Is he then still a magician? Now, suppose the magician wheels in another corpse, and all the tests are made to convince you that the corpse is indeed dead. The magician tells you tap to the forehead of the corpse. You do, and the corpse comes to life. Does that make you a magician? Do we have to know what we are doing or how we do it in order to accomplish the task?

What makes a magician magical? Isn't it, argues Macksoud, that he knows something we do not? Well, not necessarily. Can't it be that he can do something that we can't do, even though he doesn't know how he does it? These epistemological questions lead to an obvious condition of science. The scientist is not a magician; he or she must be able to explain *how* they achieved their results. Thus, they must rely on control and prediction as the sum of all knowledge. Understanding is what is left when you subtract the information yielded by control and prediction, and this understanding is an integral part of what is called "knowledge," and yet this "knowledge" may be substantially illusory.

Macksoud wants to poke a hole in the cape of respectability that we throw around scientists and, by association, social scientists. He believes it is a mistake to attribute understanding to scientists or magicians. This habit is based on the mistaken assumption that because people can *do* things we can't do, they *know* more than we do. In fact, what they may know may be rhetoric. For example, in science unlike any other profession, we accept the assumption of an orderly universe, allowing for further prediction and control. Science is either uninteresting because it produces only prediction and control, or it is interesting because it assumes a metaphysic that contradicts its method. To put it another way, the evidence of our senses does not take us by itself to knowledge; that evidence is a product of senses that can be fooled. It feels cold, but it is hot. It sounds far away, but it is near. It smells like onion, but it is garlic. Since our senses can be fooled some of the time, we ultimately have only forced generalizations from inconclusive tests and assumptions based upon past experience on which to rely. So, we fall back on probability, which means *a measure of faith is required.* Thus, the difference between astrology and science is really a matter of degree, according to Macksoud. Just listen to a few barroom conversations. "I could have guessed he was a Sagittarius. He was honest to a fault." "I should have known she was a Libra; she was so dogmatic." Experience speaks from probability that has verified pre-determined hypotheses. *We find what we are looking for.*

There is a difference that ought to be noted between understanding and what hard science reveals through apparent successes of prediction and control. Is the human eye a camera, which takes things in (merely records) or a projector that creates the images (edits, colors, and distorts)? Is it all imagination? An external reality can only be verified independent of the mind. But what is independent of the mind? What is not perceived by the mind?

Furthermore, communication is impossible without comparison. You can't describe to another person a room in which there is nothing *like* what that person has experienced. Even direct perception is comparing; we say to ourselves, "It looks *like* a rose to me." Observation, analogy, and judgment are intertwined in the act of interpretation; the making known function is thus always rhetorical. It is a matter of taking something *as* something else.

We must remember that induction always relies on memory in the verification process. Memory has a filter, and the filter may distort or edit the material recalled for inductive verification. Furthermore, as Kenneth Burke has shown, language itself imposes rhetorical filters or terministic screens on what we perceive. For almost any analogy, there is a complimentary model and dyslogistic model. The act can be "courageous," or it can be "rash," depending on the perception of the audience.

We recognize the present by comparing it to the past. Does this distort the present? Does history repeats itself? Is the future like the past? Do our experiments verify the past? The rhetorical uses of the filtered past surround us constantly and constantly determine our actions for the future. One of the objects of the massive buildup of troops before the invasion of Iraq in 2003 was to avoid the Vietnam trap, where a slow buildup became a quagmire. But once victory was declared in Iraq, troops were necessary to maintain order and secure a democratic constitution. Soon on the floor of the U.S. Senate, Senator Chuck Hagel was comparing Iraq to Vietnam; the quagmire had not been avoided after all.

Science is about counting; scientists claim to be counting to avoid being guilty of interpreting since interpreting is subjective (that is, rhetorical.) However, this strategy is flawed because before we can count something, we must characterize it, and characterization is subjective. How do we know what we are counting unless we name it? Naming must be justified rhetorically, and naming relies on analogy. Is this swine flu or not? How do you know if not by analogizing it to another case of swine flu?

In social scientific research into communication behaviors, the method becomes even more rhetorical. To measure, count, or outline patterns of behavior is to *attribute* motive to them. This is elemental in perception. Counters argue that this is justified because the motive arises out of the context. However, this is nonsense because counters don't use all of the context to determine motive since much of it is claimed to be irrelevant to their assessment. They use selected parts of the context that they assess to be relevant, hence, making a subjective judgment which requires rhetorical justification. Why is the full moon not a relevant variable to your experiment?

What is the standard for determining the relevant parts of the context? Very often it is contained the social scientist's pre-existing hypothesis. In this way, social science is tautological. *They find what they are looking for.* Furthermore, since the hypothesis comes out of past experience, it not only biases the experiment in its favor, but it re-verifies itself. Macksoud claims that the latent motive behind all of this re-certification of the past is control. Scientific description is context reliant, and contexts, much like the criteria for similarity, are plastic, that is, endlessly wide or narrow as the scientist may *choose* for particular purposes. Thus, the scientist controls the experiment.

When doing social scientific research, one can ask, what counts as a response? Isn't no response, a kind of response? Where does the ambiguity end? It ends in rationalization, and thus, in rhetorical control of the experiment. The motive in each case seems not to be the discovery of truth, but the control of the environment. In this way, Part I of Macksoud's analysis attempts to demonstrate that the scientific method is rhetorical and an attempt to bring stability, and hence, control, where much less stability actually exists.

Part II

I have spent some time on Part I of Macksoud's monograph because it is foundation to Parts II and III and helps the reader understand the subtleties of the text. The second third of the book, entitled "A Philosophic Attitude: The Illusion of the Disappearing Judge" (37 in his text which follows), attempts to undercut the grounding of logic by arguing that language is relative: "There is, I think, this persistent dilemma. *Our description becomes either explanations or commands.*" Descriptions must be edited because if they are not, they become infinite and, thus, impossible to contain. Since all things are contingent and related, one thing literally leads to another. Thus, the describers must argue for the limits they place on their descriptions. If one does not edit, the alternative is to *command* others to believe what we describe: "This is a case of swine flu."

Like Zeno and Kierkegaard, Macksoud believes that reason is inadequate for solving the problems he proposes. One must go through logic to realize its inadequacies on the way toward understanding the limits of interpretation in making sense of the world. His award-winning analysis of Ludwig Wittgenstein certainly qualified him for the next step in his argument. He aims his guns at both "ordinary language" philosophers and Logical Positivists:

> Modern objectivist linguistic philosophy combines the best devices of collectivism with some of the devices of the more evident forms of totalitarianism by assuming both popular and expert mantles simultaneously. By this ingenious device, it is made to appear that it is, in fact, *ordinary* language which is being represented (all of us, of course, are *symbolically* present at the deliberations which determine correctness of our speech) and, at the same time, that these important questions are being decided by those who are supremely qualified to make such judgments, and, in this way, to protect us from ourselves. (47-48 in his his text which follows)

Macksoud's book hopes to show that language is not up to the task of objectifying our experience. For example, he claims that the difference between analytics and metaphysics is illusory (43). Philosophy, like science, is merely elegant rhetoric because of the "boundary problems" language has; everything is metaphorical, and everything is edited. This argument reveals that Macksoud seeks to privilege rhetoric over philosophy and science. He would make them sub-fields of rhetoric. For instance, on page 45 he writes, "Many logicians, correctly anticipating the abyss, retreat from issues of reference. But surely for the rhetorician, naming is the name of the game." He goes on to claim that naming is the result of context and convention, and, thus, rhetorical and axiological, rather than epistemological (45). Therefore, Macksoud's work anticipated and, in my case, inspired developments in hermeneutics that sought to place close textual readings into phenomenologically discovered contexts and presented a critique of the sense in which that method argues for a correct reading of a text.[3]

In Part II, Macksoud also seeks to cut off the retreat into logic or linguistics. This move is important because traditionally the troika of science (informing), logic (argumentation), and rhetoric (persuasion) constitute the means to obtaining and disseminating knowledge. If Macksoud can show that each is essentially rhetorical, he reconfigures our understanding of the epistemic nature of all three. They would not have equal footing, but instead, and this is Macksoud's project, science and logic and certainly philosophy would be seen as sub-fields of rhetoric.

Macksoud begins Part II with three absurdist vignettes that demonstrate the relativity and limits of language. We need only examine the last one to demonstrate how Macksoud is previewing what is to come. In the story, a young man, who holds a bird in his hand, approaches a wise man and asks the wise one to tell him if the bird is alive or dead, while predicting that the wise man can never provide the right answer. The wise man quickly realizes that if he says that the bird is dead, the young man will allow it to fly away. If the wise man says that the bird is alive, the young man will crush it to death. So the wise man answers the questions this way: "The answer is in your hands." The pun demonstrates that literal and figurative meaning abide in the simplest of cases.

Macksoud begins by trying to show that those who split meaning from referent are trying to create a hermit language, which gives them power over nature and others. If you don't know the rules, you can't play. Here he presages Michel Foucault by arguing that this kind of linguistic knowledge gives power to those who possess it. Where Foucault reveals this phenomenon in psychiatry and criminology, among other fields, Macksoud usually reveals it in the academic community, which he came to distrust.

He demonstrates that synonymity is at the heart of language using. We agree that "bachelor" means "unmarried male," but what are the criteria for establishing a durable synonymity, and who establishes that criteria? Two methods abide. In the first, the author/speaker uses his/her authority to establishing the criteria: "As an expert, by bachelor, I mean..." In the second, the author appeals to the authority of others or a consensus of authorities: "The dictionary tells us that bachelor means..." In either case, rhetorical strategies are being employed. The first is based on ethos (the credibility of the speaker); the second is based on the logically flawed appeal to majoritarianism, consensus or other forms of established authority. Macksoud means to reveal that consensus is no more than provisional understanding, and in a second rhetorical move, each of these tactics is passed off as "objective." "What could be fairer than relying on the dictionary?" one asks rhetorically, perhaps not realizing that the dictionary is imposing the will of the majority on everyone through "consensus."

Macksoud claims that the process of naming is axiological rather than epistemic. Naming cannot be separated from valuation and, therefore, is a product of values, not solely a way of coming to know something. Naming is governed by context and convention. However, both of these methods are value weighted because context is based on perception, which can vary, and convention again relies on majoritarian consensus, a rhetorical product. Beyond that we more often rely on verbal reports to establish context and convention than we do on direct perception, removing us again from the "object" of our observation. Verbal reports insert another rhetorical layer between us and the "object" that is named. Verbal reports, as anyone watching the evening news can tell you, are colored by a point of view. Often (see Wittgenstein) this phenomenon is handled in the philosophy of language by arguing that language use is a self-contained game, and one need only learn the rules to open it up. If Wittgenstein can argue that there is a grammar of science, Macksoud can argue that there is a rhetoric of science. If there is a grammar of logic, then there may also be a rhetoric of logic, as Macksoud demonstrates when he reveals the role perception and point of view play in establishing context and convention.

This is why Macksoud warns against the formulations of those who would have us step aside and let the words do their work. Take the case of the Constitution. Macksoud does not believe that we are a nation of laws rather than men. Men and women interpret the law and often confound its original meaning. In fact, they confound its contextual meaning by changing frames and contexts. It is a very long road, rightly or wrongly, from the Fourth and Ninth Amendments to *Roe v. Wade*, which grants a pregnant woman the righ to have an abortion. It is an even longer road for the liberal minority in *Bush v. Gore* to defend the rights of states and for the conservative majority to defend judicial activism and interference in state affairs. The Constitution says what the Supreme Court decides that it says; we are a nation of humans, not laws. The justices simply need to be rhetorically adept enough to write decisions that won't get them impeached.

Language rules are constructed and only exist in operation. They are a product of perception, consensus, and inference; thus, they are open to rhetorical re-interpretation. Therefore, "our descriptions become either explanations or commands." Again, Macksoud presages Foucault by arguing it is the rule makers and interpreters that have the real power. He shows the totalitarianism latent in the behaviorists' assumption of expertise and popular consensus. They protect us from ourselves by telling us what "ordinary language" means, though the behaviorists are not ordinary at all.

Since Macksoud wrote "Other Illusions" and went into seclusion, postmodernism has corrected some of the problems he cites, but his notion that we are obsessed with order, particularly in the academic community, is not without merit even today. His reference to "linguistic health" units invokes visions of problems with endnote style, confinement to narrow fields of study, and the determination of what constitutes authority and expertise. It is not an accident that a broad and general field of study such as "communication studies" flourishes in the tolerant and teaching-oriented California State University system, but can hardly be found in anything close to recognizable form on campuses of the University of California, a "research one" institution. Where "communication studies" does exist on these elite campuses, it must defend itself by narrowing to very specific fields of study at the expense of others. It is narrowed to majors that investigate only tropology or interpersonal communication or performance studies.

Macksoud extends his argument by proving that the mythology of rule-making requires that the personal be removed. Again, while this has been corrected to some degree in the postmodern age, it is still common to see scholarly articles written with no personal reference: "This study will proceed in three stages." How does the study proceed in that manner rather than the author? The personal is obscured to render the patina of objectivity and remove the possibility that what is written is the result of human judgment, although, as postmodernism also teaches, "we"—including the author—do not definitively know who the "I" is that speaks in the name of the author.

If definitions weren't imposed on us, Macksoud argues that a "chair" could be called a "computer" because it does many things a computer does. For most of us, the sun is not just "a ball of hot gases." It is many other things that are often associated with still other things. So where has our referent gone? Macksoud hedges his bet. He tells us that he is not arguing that every chair is a computer or that you have to accept his argument that some chairs can be called computers. What he finds lacking in language philosophy is tolerance. He wants you to have the option of accepting his definition. He does not want to live in linguistic intolerance, but in a world of expanded linguistic possibilities, not unlike the "play" in language endorsed by Jacques Derrida and Francoise Lyotard.

However, if this play comes from human participation in linguistic matters, human judgment enters the picture in terms of naming in at least two ways. One must decide whether or not there is an identification (analogy) between referent and word, and one must decide whether the name will be dyslogistic or eulogistic. As Macksoud points out, there is a difference between "making love" and "screwing." These assessments are rhetorical in nature; they are hardly completely objectifiable. Furthermore, to argue that a word's relativity is limited to a "family" of meanings is no solution at all since families are infinitely expandable.

It is at this juncture that Macksoud again advances his notion of deconstruction well ahead of the time it first appeared in the United States. He writes, "Some are inclined to point to the fact that interpretation is in fact an endless process and to call uninterpretable the point at which we stop interpreting. Yet, that point is no more uninterpretable than any other simply because we stop there. Any number of extraneous factors may influence where we actually stop and the crucial question remains, at any given point, ought we to continue, since we may do so as long as we wish to" (51). Macksoud anticipates Derrida here. The critic must make a case for stopping the endless process of deconstruction. Every text implies another text, so one must make a case for the relevance of what is kept and what is bracketed out. That rationalization is clearly a rhetorical one. You must persuade your audience—academic or otherwise—that you have been comprehensive enough; you must persuade your audience that you have traced things back far enough to make your case. Lincoln's Address at Gettysburg borrows from Daniel Webster's Second Reply to Hayne and invokes laws higher than the Constitution. To deconstruct his address, one must at least go back to Webster of 1830 and to those who previously invoked higher laws. In the latter case, the search is almost infinite; in the former case, Webster of 1830 relies on his hero George Washington. Washington derived some of his ideas from Hamilton, and on it goes.

By page fifty-one, it is clear that Macksoud's argument from relativity means that he doesn't want "conventions applying themselves"; he wants us to understand that we not only have the power to construct convention rhetorically, but the power to choose which conventions to apply. For example, when we respond to a hypothetical by saying "That is impossible," we normally do not mean that the specific hypothetical is impossible; we mean that that *kind* of thing happening is impossible based on past experience, consensus, and/or expert opinion. Thus, the general rule (deduction) overrides the individual (inductive) hypothetical. It is this kind of thinking that re-enforces elegance and control but reduces the chances of new discoveries. "What if we try to develop a polio vaccine from monkey tissues?" opines Jonas Salk. "That kind of thing will never work," opines the scientific community. Luckily, Salk leans to the inductive overriding convention and produces a vaccine. Of course, as you move from the scientific world to worlds based on even lower standards of probability, conventional wisdom tends to be even less reliable. "What if the president does not move toward the center in the election of 2004, but remains defined by his conservative persona?" opines Karl Rove. "That kind of thing never works," opines the strategists. Rove relies on the inductive, overriding conventional wisdom, and the rest is history.

The bottom line for Macksoud is that we should treat "conventions," scientific or otherwise, as contingent and subjective, and thus, open to rhetorical approaches. Furthermore, since all conventions must be applied by a human mind, the conventions are attitudinally based. My attitude decides which convention I employ and even how I construct that convention. For the poetic, a paradox may be a beautiful thing, but for the logician, it is a contradiction, which is intolerable. Macksoud seeks to open the logical to individual exceptions. Thus, Macksoud's corrective advocates tolerance and skepticism. Logical and grammatical necessities are based on agreements only; thus, to call them necessities is a dangerous overstatement. When something "makes sense," it makes sense to someone. This phenomenon can be discovered in few more profound places than the jury box. What makes sense to each member of the jury is what drives them toward a consensus sought by the prosecutor, the defense attorney, or the jury foreman. Often, who tells the best story, that is, whether the prosecution or the defense makes the most sense of the facts admitted, carries the day. However, it is the best story for the particular minds and particular attitudes of that jury. Thus, the prosecutor and the defense team had best be open to (i.e., tolerant of) unique possibilities in every case.

Macksoud concludes Part II of his book with a passage from *Through the Looking Glass* in which Humpty Dumpty uses the word "glory" in a way that is unacceptable to Alice. Humpty tells her that words mean what he says they mean because he doesn't want words mastering him; he wants to master the words. Though Humpty may be wrong in various senses of that word, Macksoud "insists" that he be considered preliminarily and not dismissed out of hand. He writes, "Looked at in this way, definition is a rhetorical resource from both sides of a configuration and may be justified in a variety of unconventional ways" (55). This endorsement of rhetoric, and particularly metaphor, sets up the final section.

Part III

Part III of *Other Illusions* sates our hunger for answer to the relative and unstable world revealed in parts I and II. Macksoud warns his reader that he will advocate the rather radical strategy of tolerating at the outset any judgment of all suggested meanings. His propositions are ones of policy, not of fact. That is, he seeks to create a new attitude toward the creation of meaning and language usage. His first proposition is that the substance and forms of arguments are analogy based. Rhetorical "language using" begins with points of reference: limits, definitions, criteria. General qualitative experiences are based in adjectivals, which we try to make more and more precise under questioning. We can do this by analogizing or dis-analogizing. For example, "It felt like I was hit by a rock; it did not feel as if I was hit by a pillow." Soon, we may find that we are being led on by our own analogies or the analogies that convey meaning to others. We must admit also that if analogies can lead us they can also mislead us, and that is a danger to avoid. The problem is, if we can make the judgment that analogies can mislead us, then we must know what the correct path is. But how did we come to that judgment?

In answering this question, Macksoud seeks rhetorical instead of philosophical arbitration. That is, he wants to rely on tolerant argumentation in the present instead of formal conventions upon which agreement has been reached in the past. Thus, Macksoud would reject normative or ordinary use arguments for current or local rationales. He embraces the rhetorical stance which always asks, "*Why* is this particular convention being used? Why and how is it being justified?" In this way, Macksoud prefers the local to the general, and like many a post-modernist would avoid master narratives, which are also derived from consensus and tend to be controlling.

The application of criteria should be seen as rhetorical; that is, probable and incomplete. I tell you that a flower is a rose, and you deny it. I then apply a list of criteria to the flower: it is red, its petals are lush, it has a sweet smell, and so forth. You reply that it has no thorns, that the leaves are too shiny, and that it has too many petals to be a rose. The exchange is analogy based and rhetorical. Note the recollection of the past establishment of criteria. Your antagonist could argue, "Well, that's what we used to call a rose, but we don't call them that any longer." Or take the issue to a more sophisticated level: "Well, that's the way you define a rose; but that is not how I define a rose." These kinds of arguments are proto-typical and certainly should be justified, but how? What do we accept as justification? Doesn't that depend on our attitude? Judgments based on similarity work the same way. "You may think it is a table, but it is really a bed." "How do you know that?" The application of attributes in this case reveals that no two objects are identical, and therefore, one must argue for the application in *each* case. Thus, the shift from logical identity to rhetorical analogy is a healthy one, not unlike Protagoras's position that there are only illusions in the world; the question is how to create the most convincing one. Remember, too, that Protagoras, as an early Sophist, was very clear on the point that identity is always based on perception. Humans are the measures of all things. They take the thing for itself or for something else.

These "as" structures—as Martin Heidegger calls them—something taken "as" something, are analogous at base and pervade both inductive and deductive arguments. Examples that build inductive arguments must be shown to be similar, which requires rhetorical arguments. Applying general rules to specific cases must be justified rhetorically. Why does this rule apply in this case? Why are you applying this rule in this case?

Macksoud's second proposition is that analogies may be seen as having equal truth value. This is the case because in order for analogies to be accepted, one must accept as fact that certain attributes are similar. The criteria for establishing similarity, however, tend to be general—a rose is a rose is a rose—whereas the application of the notion of similarity to a specific case requires more convincing—this rose is a Stephen Austin rose. That application requires the judgment of a human mind, which invokes perception and thus requires convincing. At bottom then, all analogies are a rhetorical product, that is, a product of choice and the process of persuasion.

Reliance on numbers, while an attempt at objectivity, fails that test because people must agree on the number of attributes of similarity for the formula to be set in place. That agreement is based on human judgment. Furthermore, the notion of similarity presents problems for the objectivist also. How do we agree on what constitutes similarity? Agreement on measures of similarity, even when achieved, tend to be generalized and then when applied to a specific case must be examined all over again.

All objects have something in common with other objects, many of which are outside of the "normal" categories. That is why children often mistake one object for another until their sense of differentiation is matured. However, adults make the same mistake. They may mistake a poisonous mushroom for an eatable one; they may mistake a poisonous spider for a less harmful one; they may compare one war to another, leading to all sorts of disagreements. Is a terrorist attack by no more than ten individuals attributable to a nation or even a religious group? What retaliation does such an attack justify? The answers are found in analogies that generate foreign policy. To what extent was Saddam Hussein like Adolph Hitler? To what extent was the attack of September 11, 2001 on New York analogous to the attack of December 7, 1941 on Pearl Harbor?

Analogies are elastic. The right to defend one's self against physical harm gets extended to the right to defend one's country against physical harm. The right to defend one's country against physical harm gets extended to defending one's country against economic harm. (After all, should the economy be damaged, some people are going to starve.) The question becomes where and how does one cuts off these extensions. The answer is a matter of judgment and rhetorical consensus.

What we have learned about analogies can be extended to descriptions and definitions. They are not differentially correct; they are differentially persuasive. Macksoud argues that once you understand this fact, language becomes "de-objectified and de-absolutized." In this way, he seeks to restore the generative power of language. The cost may be the loss of conviction, but that may be a fair price to pay for the resulting tolerance and creativity once language is freed from is logical and scientific confines.

Macksoud's third proposition naturally follows from the foregoing analysis: "Language-using may be seen as radically strategic." Language-using is an act of choice. In fact, as I have argued elsewhere, it is an ontological constituent of human being.[4] Language-using, as Aristotle, Isocrates, Heidegger, and many more have recognized, is a defining part of our humanity. Since we communicate with others, Macksoud argues that we are engaged on a linguistic battlefield, seeking control through rationalization, seeking power through rhetoric. We hope that our illusions (truths) prevail over the illusions (so-called truths) of others. For that reason, language using should be seen as strategic.

It is also strategic in the sense that it presents edited descriptions full of chosen emphases. If you describe a rose to me, you will fail to discuss all of its contingent nature because its nature is infinite. So, your description will be partial in at least that sense and probably others. Furthermore, you will emphasize some attributes of the rose and de-emphasize others. Perhaps you will talk about its smell at the expense of the color of its leaves; perhaps you will emphasize its thorns at the expense of the length of its stems or the diseases that can attack the flower. Innocently, you may be trying to be efficient, but in being so, you are also being editorial, which is to say strategic. However, if instead of describing a rose, you were asked to describe the war in Iraq, you might begin to see how important your strategic choices can be. What Macksoud seeks is for you to lose your innocence and understand what you are doing. By understanding that you are engaged in strategic, that is, rhetorical, activity, you are less likely to become deluded and more likely to become more creative and, one would hope, more responsible when using language.

Macksoud next moves to the problem of universals. For example, how can we apply a general virtue, say generosity, to specific cases? Of course, this is a way of naming an act. What gives us the right to name it in this way? Why do we name it in this way? To name is to make an analogy in an axiological way. The analogies may not work because of similarity or even perceived similarity but succeed "only because you are persuaded that they ought to be taken as similar" (86). From the rhetorical perspective, that is, the attitude that Macksoud is advancing, all naming and all limiting is arguable. Justification is actually required; rules do not abide. Values and imagination are invoked. You understand that language use—defining, analogizing, naming— is value laden; it is axiological, and it reveals personal motives, just as Kenneth Burke taught us.

This invocation runs counter to analytic and empirical thinking. In the former case, the truth of statements is determined by rules; in the latter case, the truth is determined by observable facts. The analytic world seeks to remove language and its rules from empirical situations. The analytic world is self-contained; to enter it, a proposition must meet certain tests. Meaning is thus dissociated from experience. The empiricist would respond that all analytical statements should be empirically based, or at least that analytically derived conclusions should be empirically verifiable. *A priori* analytic propositions should be based on empirically verified, that is, repeated observations.

Macksoud explores a subtle middle ground between these positions. He claims that all statements are subject to empirical verification *and* analytical validity. The question is where they sit on the continuum between the two. How do we employ these methodologies to our best advantage? The answer lies in analogy. What parts of the proposition are analogous to empirically derived statements, and what parts are analogous to analytically derived statements? In either case, one must argue for the analogy that grounds Macksoud's method rhetorically. For example, if I make the statement that Hal cannot be in Chicago and New York at the same time, an analytical analysis will argue that laws of contradiction should be invoked, while the empirical analysis will argue that there have been no instances of a person being able to "be" in the two different places at the same time. The latter allows me to imagine exceptions; the former does not. However, in either case, I accept the statement only because I can think of no exceptions to either contention, and I can choose not to think of exceptions, because I have an agenda to advance. I like the world to be an orderly place where Hal cannot be in two places at the same time. It is this *valuing* that induces my conviction, not the other way around.

Macksoud's fourth and final proposition is that rhetoric can be seen as an end in itself. While intersubjective communication is seen by many as the goal of rhetoric, it might not necessarily be viewed that way. While communication with others is the deep and narrow view of most theorists, it is possible that other points can be found to the art. Macksoud, not surprisingly, sees one of these points as the manipulation of analogies to achieve merger or division. This is the mechanism by which we advance one perspective over another. Rhetoric teaches us that the *interpretation of evidence is more important than the evidence itself.* Macksoud's rhetoric would thus undercut the attitude of authority rather than enforce it; that again is an admonition from a lonely prophet. By page ninety, Macksoud has spent a great deal of time telling us the ways in which we should *not* be persuaded, and in the last five pages of his book, he tells us how we should be persuaded.

Conclusion

Since Macksoud's four propositions are the result of his inductive journey, it is important to see how they progress one from the other. Proposition one states, "The substance and forms of argument may be seen as analogy based." This is true, because no argument can be advanced without a point of reference, a context, which may be a definition, a criterion, or a linguistic limit (68). Each of these is based on analogical understanding. Macksoud's resurrection of analogy as the heart of rhetoric is crucial. Convincingly contextualized, and thereby well justified, analogical understanding leads us aright—the goal of Heidegger's rhetorical theory—whereas poorly contextualized analogical understanding misleads us. And those are the only possibilities in argument. Therefore, *argument is rhetorical*, that is, grounded in persuasion. Reflecting the influence of Burke, Macksoud writes, "Since all naming may be seen as identification, all descriptive statements are transformed by this perspective into statements of analogy"(73). He then praises the Sophist's insight that it is we who "determine the matter and form of identity" (74). Understanding the limits of language and argument causes the rhetorician to move beyond the dangerous hubris implicit in the denial of such limits, while the philosophers remain in denial when defending the notion that their discipline is distinct in its powers of formal logic, analytical argument, and pure description.

Proposition two argues that "analogies may be seen as possessing equal truth value," where truth value is understood as a degree of correctness or in Russell's case the degree of correspondence between language and reality. Any analogy can be viewed as in some sense "correct" depending on how plastic we make the criterion of similarity. While this proposition may certainly elevate rhetoric in general and Sophistry in particular, it may also seem to lead to academic anarchy. Macksoud bases his claim on the criterion of similarity, which he says is difficult to distinguish from dissimilarity. What looks like two very similar kinds of sand to me, are seen as very different by a Samoan. Thus, the application of the criterion of similarity is context dependent and judgment dependent. Determining to what something is similar is a rhetorical application; a question of naming or selecting an analogy, as Macksoud asserts, "…analogy itself is limited only by lack of a convincing justification which, again, I need scarcely remind you, is a matter of individual judgment" (79). In this sense, for Macksoud, the current reigning consensus of individual judgments functions as collective "knowledge" or "truth." And while these judgments are not without standards or evidence and evaluation, Macksoud's point is that neither science nor philosophy can completely eliminate the "judgment" from these assessments by reducing them entirely to self-evident calculations or mere consensus.

Proposition three asserts that "*Language-using may be seen as radically strategic*"(80). This assertion follows from Macksoud's demonstration that science, logic, and ordinary language philosophy are either inadequate to their assumed tasks or elegant rhetoric. There is no other claim in the book that rhetoricians are more likely to embrace. Like Macksoud, we believe language-using "is an act of choice" (80). It also is an editorial and, therefore, strategic act. It is ontological. The way we do it helps define who we are.

What rhetoric gains is an enormous increase in the resources at its disposal. First, because slightly altered ways of saying things lead to different perspectives and reflect different attitudes. Second, because "To the extent that language-using describes, it reduces. And to the extent that it reduces, it recommends a way of looking at something" (83).

The final proposition is that "*Rhetoric may be reformulated as an end in itself.*" This proposition is the most radical correction that Macksoud provides. Most of us who have been weaned on the Aristotelian definition of the instrumental nature of rhetoric bridle at Macksoud's claim. However, what he means—to quote him—is that rhetoric "may be used as a way of attaining stasis – or its contrary, excitation—for oneself"(91).[5] Furthermore, since science and logical convention are built on platforms of contextulization, consensus, and relativity, rhetoric can provide an alternative, self-constructed grounding in which each of us would have more confidence. Macksoud wants us to take control of the linguistic arena from the logicians, social scientists, and the ordinary language philosophers. He amplifies Protagoras' theme; there is no one truth, therefore, the one who can construct the better illusion, understood as the more convincing judgment, will carry the day. Rhetoric is the art of building the better illusion. Rhetoric undercuts certitude, but it is the most potent tool of communication in a contingent world with which one can reconstruct the world. Rhetoric produces tolerance and rewards imagination because it is skeptical and tentative. This leads to respect for the views of others, which reduces the violence that results from dogmatism. Macksoud seeks to privilege tolerance and creativity over certitude and blindly followed rules. He would resurrect the Athens of the Sophist in place of the dogmatism that killed Socrates and dominates so many minds today.

This may seem odd, since in his preface, Macksoud says that he prefers "argument to concord." However, Macksoud is highly suspicious of concord because of the ways in which it is achieved. He could not brook political correctness. He wants a free marketplace of ideas where everyone has a seat at the table, at least as long as they can defend their ideas. Those of us who were his students certainly know that to be the case. When he wrote *Other Illusions*, he said that he hoped people would attack it. Attacks he could deal with, what worried him were his defenders. So, I have undertaken this Introduction at some risk. Yet I maintain that, like the Sophists, Macksoud mandates a high degree of tolerance and prefers building the better illusion to finding the "truth." One of my favorite lines from the conclusion is inspired by Socrates: "If you will do yourself the great favor of pretending that you don't know anything, I think you may soon discover that, in many cases, you are not pretending" (93). Macksoud understands that the "generative power of language...ought to be of paramount rhetorical interest" (79). Thus, he redefines rhetoric "as the art of manipulating analogies...And...persuasion as the art of urging one perspective over another" (92). Such a stance should be highly productive of new rhetorical theory.

His rhetoric is an antidote to the "certitude and finality" of science and logic. He embraces agnosticism, as one might expect. He is forever popping bubbles, reinforcing the playful, and revealing the slippages. He resorted to other forms and went unpublished while Foucault and Derrida succeeded because while they advocate a break in form, they do not in fact break the scholarly form themselves. Macksoud's break of form might also explain why he could not engage other scholars in his conversation. Other than my two reviews, the book received no scholarly attention, despite the fact that from the late 1960s, the field of communication studies was being infected with the social scientific method. Macksoud's Philippics against this invasion were ignored, though he would have provided potent arguments for the civil war that ensued inside the discipline. The academic community in general and the field of rhetoric in particular might want to take a look at what was quashed in Macksoud's case. Even today, we do not often allow this kind of free-ranging discourse.

Macksoud celebrated rhetoric and tried to protect it against the onslaught of pseudo-science. He hoped to breed tolerance and resurrect the best of the Sophistic world, a world that was full of debate, skepticism, and creativity. After all, it was the Sophists who taught the rulers and artists of Athens, not Plato or Socrates. The contentious nature of Macksoud's rhetoric avoids final decisions, keeps doors open, and argues that there is always an alternative. Perhaps with the publication of his book by a university press, he will finally get his due.

Notes

1. Craig R. Smith, *Philosophy and Rhetoric* (Spring 1974): 113-15; Craig R. Smith, *Quarterly Journal of Speech* (December 1977): 457-58.
2. In fact, Macksoud writes, "Of course this will develop into sheer Sophistry—and Sophistry, in the sense of argument for the sake of argument, is what I shall advocate" (73).
3. See, for example, my "*Ethos* Dwells Pervasively: A Hermeneutic Reading of Aristotle on Credibility," lead chapter in Michael J. Hyde, ed., *The Ethos of Rhetoric* (Columbia:

University of South Carolina Press, 2004), 1-19. Also see Michael J. Hyde and Craig R. Smith, "Heidegger and Aristotle on Emotion: Questions of Time and Space," *The Critical Turn: Rhetoric and Philosophy in Postmodern Discourse*, Ian Angus and Lenore Langsdorf, eds. (Southern Illinois University Press, 1992), 68-99.

4. Craig R. Smith and Michael Hyde, "Rethinking the Public: The Role of Emotion in Being-with-Others," *Quarterly Journal of Speech* 77 (1991): 446-66.

5. This is not far from a position Gorgias takes in the *Encomium to Helen* where he says he often gives speeches to entertain himself.

Other Illusions

Inquiries Toward a Rhetorical Theory

S. John Macksoud

FOR JACKIE

sine qua nihil

Terse Contradiction

I

To restore rhetoric to its place; to relieve it of the burden of imitating science and logic, is what I shall essay. I do not expect that many will like that place. I like it, but my favorite weather is rain. I prefer observing to belonging, and argument to concord. I like night more than day; cold more than warmth; and silence more than most sounds. I doubt that many people occupy just this space. Indeed, I would be sorry if they did.

This catalog of tastes is intended only to suggest something of the posture from which these inquiries are made. We ought to distinguish taste from judgment, and if you do not share my tastes, I hope that you will find my judgments of interest.

II

Ease and habit are the' great killers of the mind, as disease and accident are of the body. Aside from their obvious enslavement to cultural and social institutions, our minds are in bondage to two sometimes invisible tyrants. The tyrants are kept in power by a diffuse yet adhesive praetorian guard which is pitiless in its enforcement of the tyrants' edicts. This is truly the establishment—not those who tell us which belief to hold at a particular time, but those who dictate the manner in which any belief we may hold at any time must be formed and defended. These are the rule-givers of science and logic. If images of solemn priests or of frenzied witch doctors suggest themselves, that is because scientific and logical robes are the modern habiliments of religion and magic. The robes have changed color and texture and are much more arresting to the educated eye and infinitely smoother to the knowledgeable touch, but I hope to convince you that the change is superficial and that beneath the new robes metaphysics and authoritarianism are alive and well.

The spell of the scientific method is based on the belief that it rests upon observation and control procedures which are independent of metaphysical commitment. The seat of the logician's power is the belief that by careful (and above all professional) analysis, the meaning of a linguistic collocation may be separated from its psychological associations for individuals. Each of these beliefs has an almost irresistible appeal to our desire for stability.

Just a word about negativeness: The scientist draws links among events; the logician draws conclusions from rules. Each of them permits only certain kinds of inferences and excludes (or ignores others. I take each of these to be negative attitudes, and I affirm by negating the negatives. Looked at in this way, my suggestions are both affirmative and constructive.

These inquiries deal with communication, which is neither so important and pervasive a matter as the *exhortations* of social theorists suggest, nor so simple and trivial a matter as their *explanations* indicate. It is fashionable, if not mandatory, to ground a theory of the nature and function of communication in either scientific or logical earth. I shall attempt to generate a theory of communication which avoids both ultimate grounds. There may be some question as to whether it is a theory at all, for it has neither conclusions based on rigorous testing procedures and experimental data, nor analytic lines of reason which are validated by indubitable rules of discourse. Instead, I hope to persuade you that each of these ways of doing is theoretically vapid, and I shall offer as their successor only an attitude.

III

Arguments are dispensable, but attitudes are always interesting. Most people's lexicon of attitudes is very small. In ordinary terms this is called responsibility, but responsibility is a transitive relationship. One must be responsible *to* something. In the case of the professional scholar, the responsibility is to truth, objectivity and the advancement of knowledge. My inquiries are conscientiously irresponsible. Through them runs a set of contraries; a passionate appetite for knowledge and a profound suspicion of any "constructive" step in that direction. I find the tension exciting. Many would say that both the appetite and the suspicion are excessive. Of course they are, but why would you want merely to be satisfied?

In conscientiously irresponsible inquiries, you would expect conscientiously irresponsible examples, and you will not be disappointed. The examples are of the most extreme kind, but it is difficult otherwise to advance borders of the imagination, and one can always retreat. Nevertheless, the examples may seem either frivolous or abstract to the point of irrelevance. But what seems at first to be of no practical value may seem so only because we avoid considering the implications of a reversal of a belief, because it is an inconvenience to do so. When reflection prompts modifications, we prefer to make them at the periphery of our systems.

Those few people who have been helpful have helped enormously. My debt to my students is too large to estimate. My debt to Kenneth Burke in print and in person is substantial.

Here then is simply a way of looking at some ways of looking. It is the position that I feel most comfortable arguing—and perhaps that is a rhetorical definition of belief.

I. *A Scientific Attitude: The Illusion of the Rabbit from the Empty Hat*

Not even the best magician can
produce a rabbit out of a hat
unless there is already a
rabbit in the hat.

Imagine that you go to see a magician perform and that he performs this feat: a corpse is brought onto the stage and appropriate tests are made to show that it is indeed a corpse. The magician passes his hand over the corpse and the corpse gets up, does a jig and walks off the stage.

You are incredulous. And so you go backstage and, giving the magician assurances that you will never divulge his secret, you ask how that feat is performed. And he tells you *candidly* that he has not the faintest idea.

Is he still a magician?

But you are still incredulous. Suppose that, in order to dispel your doubt, he brings another corpse onto the stage and appropriate tests convince you that it is indeed a corpse. You pass your hand over the corpse and the corpse gets up, does a jig and walks off the stage.

Does that make *you* a magician?

We want to know that we communicate. Suppose that you are in love and you tell me how it is you feel, but your description of your state produces only blank looks on my face. What do we mean by "communicate" and what is it that we communicate? Some sort of sharing is implied, but what is it that is shared?

It may be that we seek to share perceptions through language. This requires two conditions: a language which refers to percepts, and a standard way of coupling it with our sensations. It makes very little difference here whether we speak of percepts as complexes of sensations or as wholes. What is essential is that the correlation of language and experience should be reliable and that certain experiences are relatively invariably associated with certain collocations.

The ordinary way of ascertaining these associations is by correlating phenomena that are immediately perceived with the linguistic reports of others.

But suppose that I experience a sudden change in hearing, so that I now hear all tones exactly a third interval higher. This would become immediately apparent at choir practice. I am then inclined to modify my reports and to sing my part a third interval lower, but I do not then experience the same auditory percepts in the same situations as do my fellows, even though I might meet behavioral tests which would indicate that I do. You might say that the experiential differences between myself and others are unimportant, and you would be right only if you abandon the notion that it is perception which is shared in communication through language. But can we disregard experience?

We might be inclined to say that the important shared element is more structural than substantive; that we share through language outlines and relations which bind and make cohesive the percep-tual world. In ordinary terms, we might say that we share concepts.

In one sense we are on sounder ground than before, because certain variables have been eliminated by fiat. But, in another way, we are no further than before. We still lack a test to determine whether we share. (Very few are inclined to ask *why* we should test whether we communicate—only *how*. There is, in what I am about to say, an assumed lack of faith. If you are willing to say that you *just* know that we communicate, what I have to say in this discussion will interest you only as play therapy.)

* * *

What sorts of tests will be appropriate for our purposes? We might generate linguistic descriptions of a phenomenon and look for congruences among the descriptions, but if we choose this manner of testing, we must *already* have standards for what will count as differences and similarities among the descriptions, for it is extremely unlikely, and perhaps even undesirable from the viewpoint of organisms who value variety, that we will get identical descriptions. This lack of uniformity would hardly be conclusive evidence that we do not share concepts. But this raises the question of whether we ought to regard congruence among the descriptions as presumptive evidence that we do share concepts Might we, for example, be attending to different phenomena and using an identical description, as when the heroine in a film is referring to features of the landscape and the suitor assents to them as references to her anatomy. But surely we can take measures to insure that no such bizarre situation intrudes on our tests.

What is required to eliminate the possibility of perceptual equivocation? We want to say that ordinary experimental controls can eliminate obvious and gross perceptual ambiguities, and I will want to say a great deal about this matter. But what I want to establish now is that a necessary, if not a sufficient, test of communication is the isolation of a stimulus-response pattern. Thus, even if, as conceptualists, we consider stimulus-response patterns inadequate to establish or account for concept-sharing through language, we will have to admit that they cannot be absent from our paradigm of communication, for any paradigm based neither on faith nor *at least* on stimulating responses would be clearly inadequate to establish the sharing aspect of communication.

It may seem that the emphasis here is on human behavior, but don t you see that all tests are behavioral, and that if you abandon human behavioral tests, you will have to replace them with tests of other sorts (chemical, or what you will). Even for the most radical conceptualist, any test must be behavioral.

Even if you assent to the principle of the stimulus-response pattern, you may wish to argue that response need not be overt and there seem to be several cases which we would want to call communicative configurations that wouldn't necessarily involve overt responses. But I ask you to consider whether these situations ought to be used as models, since, if we admit one such to the paradigm level, we may find it difficult to distinguish it from cases in which persons talk to inanimate objects and allege that they are heard and understood by them. I think that we are bound to response as an essential index of communication.

What is involved in the stimulus-response paradigm? To what burden of proof do we commit ourselves? I want to show you that the stimulus-response pattern is inescapably causal—roughly in the Aristotelian sense of efficient cause—and that it will not tolerate reduction from connection to correlation. To call a piece of behavior a response is to imply that it was elicited and to speak of stimulating a response is to speak of a connection, not a correlation. To draw a stimulus-response pattern is to say more than that a certain sort of behavior is highly correlated with another occurrence. For example, when you say that two persons use the same word in the same situation, you imply that they use the word in response to the same stimulus—otherwise, what does *same situation* mean? Thus, if we speak of communication as at least stimulating responses, we definitely imply a causal connection. I will want to show that, in the rules for isolating operative stimuli, there is a set of metaphysical premises.

* * *

For no very good reason except that their resolution is inessential to the making of my case, I propose to dispense with some possible sources of difficulty by granting certain assumptions. These are provisional assumptions without which we could not operate further, and I want to grant them in that way—provisionally, not finally.

First, I propose to grant that a given stimulus, which is hypothesized as operative, can recur. Thus, I will grant that a stimulus can be treated as a member of a uniform class, rather than as a unique particular. Without this stipulation, stimuli would be unrepeatable, and no two tests could be explained by a single operative stimulus. (For other reasons which I shall develop later, I will not grant this uniformity to scientific tests taken as wholes; indeed, the uniformity problem is in part what leads me to posit an analogical base for relations among different tests.) I also want to assume that there are no independent internal operative stimuli, nor indeed any stimuli which are unobservable in the context of the test conditions, for otherwise, there could be no control or measurement of a large body, perhaps infinitely large, depending upon our method of counting, of possible operative stimuli. This immediately shows you that the statistician's canon, "if it exists, it is measurable," is a definition of existence rather than a statement about instrumentation.

The problem that confronts us in communication testing is to isolate the operative stimulus of a given response. We must answer the question: "What actually elicits a given response?" For only in this way can we compose our contention that we communicate. Our problem, then, is to determine whether we communicate in a particular case—to determine what works.

Scientists never correctly predict the future. They merely predict that the past will recur. We don't have a case of *correct* prediction at all until a communicative configuration has already taken place. Thus, if we say that we predict *correctly*, we can only be said to have predicted the past, i.e., the label "correct" can only adhere *after the fact*.

I want to argue that only by repetition do we generate explanations in a scientifically satisfactory way, that we cannot repeat the past and that our confidence in matched groups of subjects or conditions, or both, is pure metaphysics, given our capacities to observe and control. (The word "metaphysics" has many uses. Here I only use it to mean that which is beyond what can be ascertained by empirical observation.) I want to argue then, that the adhesive of our explanations and predictions is analogical argument.

And it is no good saying that we don't want to explain, but only to describe or cite correlations. Such "descriptions" are invariably selective and incomplete. For any given event everything is perfectly correlated; and for repeated tests, we "describe" only *some* of the highly correlated items. For instance, you won't allow just *any* set of correlations (e.g., that subjects are wearing white underwear on several tests) to count as relevant correlations to a communicative configuration. So we are seeking, explicitly or otherwise, what are called *relevant* correlations.

* * *

Perform and repeat this experiment. Ask a willing and capable subject to make a fist and observe his response. Let us suppose that he performs an operation which satisfies the command. We are inclined to say that the verbal stimulus elicited the behavioral response. I want to show that our confidence in such tests is metaphysically grounded in at least three ways. Two of these reach beyond our control of experimental variables, and the other, a ubiquitous principle of scientific interpretation, reaches into an epistemological void which only human will can fill.

Suppose that you allege that the verbal command stimulated the response, but I argue that it was the presence of a shadow falling across the subject's face. Repeating the test—and I do not mean to say that we could do so without altering *anything*—would be useless. I suppose that you will want to remove the shadow and produce the response again. Suppose that you do. On this test, I hypothesize that it was the pinch of a tight left shoe that caused the response. Very well, you will remove the left shoe, and reproduce the response. But on this test, I hypothesize that it was a cramped position of the coccyx that produced the response. Let me suppose that you will run out of patience before I run out of hypotheses. What are we to do? On what *ground* are we to prefer the verbal stimulus to the other hypothesized stimuli? It is clear that we must now state grounds upon which hypotheses *should* be accepted. But, n.b., if we do, we reduce the question to one of persuasiveness.

You are perhaps inclined to attempt a fool's mate by asking why such conditions as I have pointed to *should* influence the response. But I counter with the question why the *verbal* stimulus *should* have relevance. Now I suppose that you are inclined to invoke *past experience*, the *nature* of the various physical mechanisms involved (the ear, coccyx, etc.) or both. But how was their "nature" established and how did you interpret past experience? Wasn't it in just the same way that is now being challenged? You will have to seek some more painstaking proof.

Clearly the method of eliminating other possible causes until only your hypothesized stimulus remains will fail, given my inexhaustible supply of hypotheses. Perhaps you will try a method of concomitant variations. You may run several tests, some with, and some without, the verbal stimulus. And you may find that the response occurs *only* on those tests with the verbal stimulus and *never* on any test without it. But suppose that I now offer an alternative explanation. Suppose that I hypothesize that on the first test where the verbal stimulus was absent the lack of response should be explained by the presence of a cinder in the subject's right eye (or yours, or mine, or God's) and that, on the second test without verbal stimulus, the operative stimulus that was withheld was an upright position of your palm (or the subject's, or mine, or God's).

Nonsense! Yes, but don't you see that we are *both* talking non-sense.

It may be unnecessary to specify the nonsense I am talking, but it is important that you see that your interpretation of these tests also goes beyond sense in three ways. First, the tacit assumption is that you can test and control all of the possible operative stimuli. No, you want to say that it is not necessary to test all *possible* variables, but only those which are *relevant* to the response in question. But remember that the criteria for relevance (past experience or the nature of the situation's elements) was derived in just the way I am here questioning, so that at some time you made purely arbitrary exclusions, unless you have in fact tested all *possible* hypotheses.

Second, we have been talking very glibly about eliminating variables. This suggests that it is possible to reduce the *total* number of variables that may be relevant (and, further, that once eliminated, a variable can *never* have been relevant). But surely we oughtn't to speak in this facile way of eliminating variables. For depending upon how we count, we must, in *eliminating* a shoe as a variable, *introduce* a bare or thinly covered foot. Our control processes have limits.

But by far the most significant metaphysical premise in the standard scientific process of explanation is the notion that if a single variable is conspicuously present in several tests it is to be preferred as an explanation to several different variables, each of which occurs in only one test. But, surely, the issue here is what elicits the response in *any given case*. And the relevance of the emphasis on repetition of a single stimulus on *different* tests is not immediately apparent. Why do we insist upon *generalizing* in this way?

Two short justifications for an insistence upon this sort of explanation come to mind. It may be that it is more aesthetically pleasing to reduce the number of variables to which one attends, and not to have to clutter our charts with too many different items. Scientific simplicity may be a mask for aesthetic simplicity. But this is no epistemological justification.

Or you may be inclined to argue that it is simply more convenient to reason in this way, but, if I ask "convenient for what?" I am likely to get, as an answer, "convenient to generalize." And then if I ask, "why do you wish to generalize?" I may very well be answered, "because it is convenient." This grows tiresome.

Perhaps you think the entire argument trivial in either importance or in extension. I will discuss the former objection later, but, preliminarily, I want to say that if we cannot ground communication theory in causal relations, we have no real basis for talking of persuasion or rhetoric in any but the most subjective way. Since, although I have been treating the problem of causality in a communicative configuration from the standpoint of observer, the problem is not mitigated by taking the position of responder or subject, for even in this position, we cannot isolate operative stimuli except subjectively.

As to the extension of the argument, I have difficulty setting limits upon its application, for even where we are not dealing with an obviously causal hypothesis (where we say we are only generating descriptions) there is still an implicit causal argument, as when we say that water boils. To describe is usually to generate a causal argument.

Indeed, in the most profound way, all descriptions of phenomena must hypothesize that some physical (ontological) event causes the perceptual (epistemic) event. Of what are our descriptions descriptive?

We may also ask this sort of causal question of the frequently used argument that justifies science on the basis of the things that the scientific method produces. Suppose that we had not invented penicillin or birth control pills or space vehicles. What is there to say that we would not have had a drop in the persistence of certain types of infections (including pregnancy) or that we would not have reached the moon on just such-and-such a day at just such-and-such a time anyway? How can we know where a road we didn't take at a certain time would have taken us?

Thus, our faith in testing would appear to be based upon a *determination* (for whatever, if any, reason) to generalize at all epistemological costs. I take this to be exemplary of the suffusion of psychology in metaphysics and as a vindication of psychologies which are based on human will.

* * *

Is there a primitive concept of probability which this analysis ignores? What do we mean by probability? What is *its* foundation? We are inclined to say that probability is a rough measure of our confidence that a given sequence of events will remain constant, or that it will vary in constant ways, but this is so patently a subjective standard, and so obviously subversive to our desires for science, that we invent mathematical indices for occurrences. This seems to justify and objectify our feelings of confidence. But before we can chart probabilities we must *select* the phenomena to be charted. One might expect that this selection would be drawn from a universe of great breadth, but, in fact, our selection is bounded by what we call past experience (which is sometimes expressed as judgment predicated upon the nature of things). But surely to justify a present interpretation by an invocation of past experience which was accumulated by the method in question is to invoke a self-validating truth. And surely these judgments rely upon analogical reasoning in much the same submerged way as there is an analogy necessary in the use of introspective evidence on any intersubjective point.

The plastic nature of interpretation and memory helps us to reinforce perceived frequencies. And the lack of criteria for selection allows negative cases always to be accounted for facilely.

Probabilities are based upon frequencies which we select. (I have never understood why it is the verbal processes of psycho-analysis that are thought so relevant to cures produced by twice-a-week, hour-long sessions for two or more years on the analyst's couch, when it seems so eminently reasonable that if, instead, one were to lie down perfectly quietly for an hour twice a week anywhere, one would feel better after a couple of years, and be so much more affluent.) Still, high frequencies seem persuasive, both in forming our own judgments and in convincing others. And if we ask why, we may again fall into the vicious circle of frequencies leading to probabilities which are based upon fre-quencies which lead to probabilities, etc. But not necessarily— there is one more depth of justification.

* * *

What is it that distinguishes scientific causal argument from simpler or more primitive *post hoc ergo propter hoc*? What makes frequent couplings of events persuasive? It is not an empirical argument, but a principle of interpretation. Probability and frequency are the children of *elegance*. Indeed, they may be elegance itself in disguise. (One is never quite certain in these cases of family resemblance.) They are never seen together because they reside at different epistemic depths. If causal arguments rest upon some notion of probability, and frequencies compose probabilities, then at the bottom of the epistemological column of science is elegance.

Consider what *principle* directs our selection of hypotheses as to operative stimuli. Past experience is material rather than itself a method of explanation. (Surely past experience must be selected from.) We need a principle to transcend sense, and we have it: *We will prefer the simplest explanation; we will not multiply entities beyond necessity*. It seems that this principle naturally leads us to prefer the common factor in repeated test situations, rather than to introduce the complication of a different stimulus in each case, but I am unsure that even this principle necessarily leads to the conclusion that science desires without the superimposition of an attitude or predisposition.

We prefer the simplest explanation. The simplest for what? The simplest to explain. As in: the fittest will survive. The fittest for what? The fittest to survive. The judgment is, of course, made after the fact. Any organism which survives is fittest and any explanation which explains is preferable. But preferable to what? Preferable to explanations which don't explain? But in each case introduced earlier, other hypotheses explained as well as the verbal stimulus. Only there was something missing; the collectibility of the many cases.

And as for the principle which directs us not to multiply entities beyond necessity, surely the point at issue here is just exactly what is necessary, as opposed to accidental, in each case. What interpretation of Ockham's principle is really being invoked? We have no real criteria for either simplicity or necessity which tell us to prefer the common stimulus in repeated cases. Surely one reading of *simplest* could be one explanation for each test and surely there is a kind of *complexity* about crossing test cases with a single explanation. And neither version of necessity multiplies entities, for the same number of entities is present in either version in each case, and only one is being identified as an operative stimulus. (Although it is indeed difficult to see why God-and-the-verbal-stimulus couldn't be taken as a *single* entity. Do we have criteria for separability of entities?)

Ockham's razor has another interpretation that is appropriate to

an electronic age. It may be taken as a principle of economy
without counting the cost. But even here one might argue that the
cross-explanation step with a single common factor is not
economical unless there is a later reward. And of course there is.
Ultimately this step enables us to generalize without testing at all.
That is the only felicity (if such it is) of the scientific method.

* * *

The strict utilization of the law of parsimony leads me to two
methodological questions. Does the application of a principle of
selection for a desired purpose count as an inductive method? And
does this approach provide a metaphysic-free method of examining the empirical world, or is it merely a different metaphysic
from the orthodox religious or magical metaphysic? For it is clear
that elegance, in the sense of brute economy, rules the scientific
world as a God-principle, since it dictates both the ways in which
data will be interpreted and the sorts of models which will be
acceptable.

So strongly does elegance hold our minds that, here, you may
say that I can't ask you to abandon a principle without giving you
an alternative principle, but the fact that you ask for a principle
only shows that you demand an equally *elegant* procedure.

Yet one can hardly deny the utility of such a principle. It is
only elegance which enables us to say that the earth revolves
around the sun rather than the sun around the earth; that the
earth is spheroid rather than trapezoidal; and that the shining sun
makes the crops grow rather than the inverse.

And if you are here inclined to point to the fact that I behave
elegantly in many cases, I remind you that it requires elegance on
your part to make this observation, i.e., it is only elegant behavior
by elegant interpretation, just as my description of the way the
scientist operates assumes that the cause of his performing in
certain ways is always because he observes elegance. Clearly, he
may operate as he does for a variety of different causes, for of
course he could predict correctly without elegance. I have created
a paradigm scientist. And if my description of elegance itself is
itself elegant, *tu quoque* will not answer here. If I tell you that
there is a black widow spider on your neck, are you really more
comfortable if there is one on mine as well?

Elegance is the enabler of generalization, and generalization is the apology for elegance. Thus generalization as a *product* is the child of elegance, and as a *motive* is its father. Not even the best magician can produce a rabbit out of a hat unless there is already a rabbit in the hat.

* * *

What exactly is the use of generalizing? Isn't it that a generalization enables us to set a limit? Remember that a limit has two sides, so that certain cases are included and certain cases are excluded. Since we know that generalizations cover *likes*, rather than *identities*, the fundamental process of generalization may be seen as one of analogy and dysanalogy. Isn't this a rock bottom of the method, and isn't generalization the process upon which scientific procedures hinge? Only by analogizing and dysanalogizing can we begin to exercise "control" or "predict." Thus, I take it that analogy is the adhesive of generalization. By analogy I mean here a process of reasoning which is logically or psychologically (I can never quite distinguish them) implied *before* a generalization can be made. It is difficult to say whether the process is conscious and willed, or habitual, or automatic.

We sometimes speak of causality as *invariable sequence*, but *invariable* and *sequence* are themselves analogies. (Does the sun come up in just the same way each day?) Thus, not only the notion of causality, but also the identities of its constituents are based upon analogies.

* * *

I suppose that such scientific tests might have several purposes, but they all seem to cluster about the same center—prediction and control. (I am never just sure which is a preliminary step toward the other. It may be a question of temperament rather than of either scientific method or of ad hoc purpose.) For these ends there is but one appropriate test, and one ultimate justification—*it works*!

One can hardly deny that success succeeds (although I shall wish to raise several questions in connection with the matter of how we count and account success).

I want to show you that elegance is built into our way of explaining the phenomenon of scientific prediction. The enterprise of using acts of repeated correct prediction as an apology for the scientific method is predicated upon viewing the acts of prediction while *already* using an elegant explanation. We are in awe of the ability of science to predict correctly, but anybody can predict correctly. Thus, what impresses us is that science predicts correctly so frequently, but must the reason for the correct predictions of science always be the *same* reason rather than several different independent reasons. An explanation of an act of prediction is a piece of stimulus-response reasoning and it requires all of the assumptions of that kind of reasoning. Where are we? The argument for elegance is repeatedly correct prediction, but our explanation of correct prediction rests upon elegance (and of course such a question may be raised with equal justification in regard to scientific *control*).

The scientific viewpoint is rooted in the metaphor of a continuing stream of kinds of connections (Doesn't this make clear that something more than correlation is being sought?) and there is nothing wrong with that, if, for whatever reason, your purpose is to generalize. I wonder only if it is candid to characterize this as a method of observation.

* * *

What do we mean when we say of an act of communication that it works? There is an ambiguity to be resolved. Our judgment may be either epistemological or axiological. Or perhaps I should say that it may be axiological, but it must be epistemological, since whatever you may argue about the extent to which it is necessary and desirable that we *should* have a communication-based *weltanschauung*, first it will be necessary that you should be able to isolate, and identify convincingly, just what *it* is that *works* to produce a particular response in a particular case. And that is, of course, precisely what I have been arguing is impossible with purely empirical means.

As operationists interested in control, we are inclined to ask for something that works *better* before abandoning an apparatus. But I ask you what that something new must be *better than*, since we do not know what is now operant (and remember that we cannot repeat a situation in which "it worked" *exactly*). In other words, our control of communicative configurations may be either illusory or metaphysically constituted, or both (I am using *metaphysical* here to mean above or beyond empirical data.) and is certainly grounded in the processes of analogy and dysanalogy.

But I know that the fact that you can predict a certain response correctly is still echoing in your mind. This only illustrates that we are frequently so dazzled by how much we can *do* that we conveniently forget how little we *know*.

What does the word "know" mean here? Am I seeking more than there is? I hope to have made a case that to the extent that scientific tests are taken as explanations they are metaphysically grounded, but it is entirely possible that I am radically miscon-struing the intent and use of science (although it is difficult to ignore the usual applications of scientific tests as explanations with which natural and social sciences are riddled). Perhaps it is not the intention of the scientist to explain at all. Indeed, one interpretation of scientific method is that explanation is one of the functions which is systematically closed to science. And many scientists would insist, further, that to require more of science than prediction and control is to ask that a fine grandfather clock should also have a cuckoo. Perhaps we should value science not, as we are inclined to do, because it can do so much, but rather because it can do the little it does so well. Or perhaps we should distinguish between a *hard* science, which would limit itself to observable correlations, and a more speculative *soft* science, which would encompass explanation.

Imagine that you go to see a magician perform and that he performs this feat: a corpse is brought onto the stage and appropriate tests are made to show that it is indeed a corpse. The magician passes his hand over the corpse and the corpse gets up, does a jig and walks off the stage.

You are incredulous. And so you go backstage and, giving the magician assurances that you will never divulge his secret, you ask how that feat is performed. And he tells you *candidly* that he has not the faintest idea.

Is he still a magician?

But you are still incredulous Suppose that, in order to dispel your doubt, he brings another corpse onto the stage and appropriate tests convince you that it is indeed a corpse. You pass your hand over the corpse and the corpse gets up, does a jig and walks off the stage.

Does that make *you* a magician?

What is it that makes the magician magical? Isn't it just exactly that he knows or understands something that we do not? If you say that the magician is a tool in the hands of an outside force then why wouldn't you say that of the scientists as well (but then you could not call him a scientist, for "science" means "to know")?

Does everything there is to know here lie before us? For it is just this posture which hard science would have us adopt: the posture that prediction and control is all there is to knowledge. If you want to know what I mean by knowledge, subtract what is yielded by prediction and control (and that yield doesn't necessarily include the confidence that your powers will persist) and what is left is what I will call understanding, and is what I think we should regard as an integral part of knowledge. Later I will discuss whether that understanding must be intersubjectively verifiable, for despite strong contrary persuasion, reinforcement from others seems to me not necessarily a condition precedent to all personal conviction.

Yet even though there is no reason to attribute understanding to those who can predict and control (both the magician and the hard scientist abandoned you at that door) it is still evident that we do so, and this may produce the illusion of knowledge and of potency when it is viewed from the balcony. Of course there may be a marked difference between our perceptions from the audience and a personal interview with the scientist, and as in the case of the magician, the scientist may be resolute in his disclaimer of knowledge in our sense. It is, after all, a question of attitude.

But the dilemma persists. If we take science to explain, rather than to simply predict and control, its metaphysical bone structure is noticeable. This encompassing metaphysic is some- times cavalierly dismissed as the assumption of an orderly universe. (It is true that you have to start somewhere, but try to get an equivalent assumption granted for any other profession. I do not see that some assumptions are more equal than others; after all, if you grant the core assumptions of any viewpoint, scientific or otherwise, all else will follow.) In fact, the foundation of science is so much more than the assumption of an orderly universe. It is the assumption of a universe which fits our preconceptions, is orderly in the same way as that order which seems to be demanded by science, and is controllable and predictable with meager means.

Thus, to the extent to which science is regarded as providential of knowledge, it ought to be regarded as metaphysical. And to the extent to which it *only* predicts and controls, it may be taken as relatively uninteresting for the understanding of phenomena. It seems either to provide too much for its own terms (i.e., that it can't sustain its claim to metaphysical abstinence) or too little for us. Does it require less faith—or even a different kind of faith—to accept the results of scientific tests than that amount required to sustain any introspective or intuitive belief? (By *faith* I only mean a continuous or consistent belief in some essential aspect of existence which underlies actions.) It may be that magic and religion cannot work absent a willing suspension of disbelief—but then it may be that nothing does. And, with that suspension, any of them surely will work, for of course there is always a scientific explanation for everything, if that is the sort you prefer. There is nothing which can't be accounted for by any system.

What I am here arguing is that the evidence of our senses does not by itself take us as far as knowledge. The ordinary metaphysical attack upon science is that it fails to attain certainty, but I do not question it because it fails to produce certainty but because the whole notion with which it replaces certainty is equally metaphysical. What I am after is not the abandonment of science, but that the scientist should be eternally, if only dimly, connected with an angel who periodically tugs at his hair and forces him to look upward and way, "Me too; yes, me too."

Examine the assumption of an orderly universe alongside the occult belief that the universe is a cohesive unit. May not such a unit be symbolized either by tarot cards or by scientific tests? It is only that different sorts of events have significance (and confidence in the predictions of the one or of the other must still involve a causal argument based on an analogy).

Is it because Empiricus is identified as the physician, and seems to produce cures without faith, that the metaphor has held our minds so rigidly? There is undoubtedly a sense of security that accompanies scientific testing (which is only a paradigm for all testing), but it cannot be that need alone that motivates the testing, since we could and do have feelings of security without testing in some cases. It seems rather that the testing satisfies a more specific need for security through generalization and, in turn, through analogy. This may give us a feeling of union with others. I am by no means suggesting that feelings of security, illusory or not, are *malum in se*. Illusions do not necessarily harm more than they help. I only want to suggest that there may be a radical difference between what hard science yields and understanding.

I did not suppose that you would be inclined to argue that the power to perform an act is *in all cases* cognate with the understanding of that act, but there is the entirely respectable and professional attitude that performance is all that *matters* (n.b., all questions seem ultimately to dissolve into questions of attitude) and that to look for more from our minds signifies a weak grasp of reality. If you ask me what more is to be found, I confess that I am unable to set before you a metaphysical banquet. It is only that I am not prepared to abandon the possibility that you may be able to lay your own table richly that causes me to urge that you make no final settlement for a moderate meal. Whether there is more to be found or not is a genuinely interesting question, but however it may be, it is only we who can answer the question. Ontological limits need not necessarily be mental limits and who is to say which determines which. That is not the point at issue here. It is rather our *willingness* to make the settlement which seems to me to impoverish us in some respects

Not even the most fertile metaphor—and who can deny the fertility of the scientific *weltanschauung*—will bear spinning out indefinitely and exclusively to people of imagination and curiosity. (Oddly, our modern *mythos* seems to conjoin an attitude of curiosity only with the scientific enterprise.)

After all, it is a question of temperament. And it is by no means clear just what expressions correlate with what kinds of attitudes. For instance, I suspect that it is the hard scientist who really has the weak grasp on order, and is institutionalizing his need of it, Just as I suspect myself of having too strong a belief in the fixity of things. A man's philosophy may be a prayer for surcease from his beliefs, for the repeal of his temperament, but however wise may be our secret magic, it is the folly of our public reasoning by which we are known.

* * *

Is the human eye the eye of the camera or of the projector? Is the ear microphone or loudspeaker? Are our senses windows on the world or mirrors of an inner order? Or, rather to put it more interestingly, can we draw a picture entirely from imagination, or can we draw it from anything else? Is there no other way to begin but with a question of analogy?

It seems we cannot answer the question of whether there is an external reality independent of the mind precisely because the specific information required would have to be obtained by some method independent of the mind. Thus we are inclined to reject the question, or at least to ignore it. But ought we to regard a question simply as an incomplete answer, i.e. as something that can be completed by specific and already properly classified information, for if we do, we eliminate all sorts of occasions upon which some people find it necessary to inquire. If we are inclined to reject the question of an independent reality on the ground that it involves a dilemma or a paradox (dilemma if we regard it as an empirical problem, paradox if as an analytic one), we should remember that, "What is the wave length of an electron having a certain velocity?" would have been a meaningless question for a Newtonian physicist to ask.

* * *

Imagine that you awaken to find yourself in a place where no aspect of the environment bears any resemblance to anything you have ever known. What would guide you? The satisfaction of various needs, physical or intellectual, may first occur to you, but before you can begin to answer my question, you will have to ask me, "If the world in which I find myself is totally unlike any I have known, what is it like?" This immediately shows us that there is something radically wrong with the original problem, for how can I answer your question? Only with a comparison, and this is precisely what is denied you in the problem. But how can it be denied you *in fact*?

Indeed, I could not even pose the problem without using some comparison. I wanted to say, "Suppose you find yourself in a mysterious room." But that would have suggested several cues. I could not pose the problem without a comparison partly because a problem implies a statement in language—which cannot help but suggest comparisons—and partly because our processes of perception may be radically comparative, for in looking at the immediate phenomena about us, there may be instantaneous comparisons implied. Otherwise, what is meant by perceiving that you are in a room rather than in a wood, and as soon as those processes begin, the room is no longer mysterious.

If our perceptual processes are radically comparative in this way, what then follows concerning a method founded upon observation and sense perception? One immediate result is that we may see that observation and analogy are intertwined (and so is judgment itself) and of course we are inclined to say that observation is informed by our past experiences. This seems to leave the inductive method intact. We are still inclined to say that it is our sense perceptions (mediate or immediate) alone which ground our conclusions.

But I ask for introspective candor in response to two questions. Is it really past *sensations* which we remember, or is it relatively cohesive *amalgams* of these? And is it *all* past experiences which bear upon an immediate observation? An answer to the first question must turn upon what we count as memory, and what we count as one memory rather than several, but it ought to be intuitively apparent that it is not *all* of our past experiences, however constituted, which bear upon a present interpretation, except in some vague philosophical way. This implies an organizer or filter which selects and directs perceptions. Call that filter what you will, its admission to the paradigm of observation is the pivot upon which the question of the objectivity of our perceptions turns because we are forced to ask to what extent our stimulus patterns, in particular cases, are governed by the filter, and furthermore, to what extent the filter is capable of alteration by immediate sensation.

It has been fashionable in the intellectual community, ever since the general rejection of radical empiricism, to think that the answer to this question involves a very subtle and delicate interplay, but this seems to me no more reasonable or defensible than that the answer should be unequivocal and absolute. Is it really more probable that the world is gray, rather than black and white?

* * *

When we say that the future will be like the past, what are we saying? What sort of judgment is this? First and most obviously it presupposes the act of comparison in our perceptions, regardless of the posture we may take on the issue of just what is being compared. But it says much more. For in looking at the present, how can you compare it with the past and find no similarity. In the comparison process some similarity is implied. How could we recognize the present if it were *totally* unlike the past? Of course the future and the present must be like the past, but elements of the external world need not be similar, for in any case we would insist on the continuity. And this may be taken either as a *definition*, i.e. not as a sense expectation, but as a determination to admit no imaginable instances in which the future is unlike the past, or as a record of our determination to compare and so to find analogies and dysanalogies. Both analogies and dysanalogies are absolutely essential: analogies, in order that comparison should be *possible*, and dysanalogies, in order that comparison should be *necessary*.

In any case, the statement that the future will be like the past operates as a law, and it is we who make the laws. I do not propose to discuss whether it is language, some psychological Gestalting process, or wires in the hands of God too thin to be noticed which causes us to perceive as we do. Select your own hypothesis. I shall arrest my tendency to speculate on this point, since any proof would be subject to the critique of testing which I have outlined, and thus metaphysical. All that I hope to have established is that the perception and interpretation of immediate data involves some process of expressed or implied comparison.

* * *

I want now to explore the question of the limits of the process of perception and of the "laws" of perception and observation. How are we to interpret the behavioral results and components of our communication tests? We have been talking as if our only problem were to establish causal relations and as if we could proceed unhampered if only we did establish (by fiat, faith, or tenacity) such connections. Presumably, we would then get on with the business of science, which is, after all, counting. We tend to take the quantitative method as a solution to the problem of interpreting behavior. We will not *interpret*, we say, we will simply count. The efficacy of this reductive process is roughly parallel to the attempted reduction of causal connections to correlation, but for a very different reason, since, whereas the reduction of causal connection to correlation attempted to omit the last step of the process (which alone gave the process point), the reduction of behavior to quantitative units attempts to omit the first step of the process. For surely *before* we can *quantify* behavior, we must *characterize* it; that is, we must establish some limits as to what will count for us as the stimuli and responses which we seek to measure and count. Before we can determine whether a subject responds with three taps, we must first know what counts as a tap, and what counts as only one tap. If it seems to you that this problem can be solved by instrumentation, substituting, for instance, a lever to be pushed for a tap, ask yourself candidly whether you can always distinguish a push from an involuntary muscle movement and what tells you which is more probable. Isn't it past experience and the nature of the mechanisms?

I insist that the problem of identification and characterization is antecedent to all questions of measurement and counting. We have no sense impressions of units of measurement apart from that which is being measured, whether it is a unit as precise as a millimeter, or as general as a response. I leave aside the obvious problem that in many cases our method of counting gives us no idea of the intensity of a response, which may, for some purposes, be important.

The process of counting proceeds from the material to be measured. And quantification, the panacea for all descriptive ills, is not even a preliminary solution to problems of characterization and cannot therefore objectify perceptions. Before we can count, we must first know what it is that we are counting. Otherwise, how will we know what counts as one and only one unit?

Of what use is it to say that we have a uniform mathematics if it need not be *applied* uniformly? If you can be persuaded that the substances which we seek to quantify are perceptual and linguistic plastic to which the process of measurement can be applied in various correct ways, not only will the whole process of interpretation be hued differently, but some interesting by-products will be evident. As, for instance, it will follow that there can be no importance in lucky or unlucky numbers—by counting the fat lady as two people, we are not thirteen for dinner—and that predictions will come as true as we wish them to.

* * *

The kinds of substances to be measured, in ordinary cases of communication, are human behaviors. I want to show you first that, in a strong sense, to measure and perceive patterns of behavior, or even discrete units, is to attribute a motive to the behavior which may exceed the character of the simple stimulus-response pattern; that in a large number of cases, knowing or inferring a stimulus-response pattern implies another intermediary step which is not *necessarily* contained in the character of either the stimulus or the response; that, in these cases, the attribution of a motive is *elemental* in perception.

Consider for example whether a feeling of sadness when a child groans with pain—which might register on a polygraph in roughly the way in which a response to the nude image of a beautiful woman or to a blow in the stomach would—is inferable *just* from the stimulus of the groan. Aren't there complex intermediary motives involved in just interpreting its character? Indeed, can you think of significant cases in which there is no element of motive in the characterization of some sequence of human behavior? And if so, can you contrive useful and significant *applications* of the behavior which don't presume some motive pattern? Isn't the inference process in perception inextricable from the question of motive? And isn't it just that step which we found to be ubiquitous from the *onset* of perception?

If there is a more or less hidden attribution of motive in the process of perception, we must ask how we determine motive in human behavior. We want to say that we follow the legal model of reasoning which tells us to determine the motive of an act from the character of the act itself. The question of motive in many criminal acts is automatically constructed by the law on the basis of the act itself. But if we examine the manner in which we ordinarily construe an act, we find that inferred motives are instrumental in the way in which we characterize or perceive it. Do I then correctly understand us to be saying that inferred motives constitute a necessary part of the way in which we perceive behavior and that we infer those motives from the behavior which we perceive? Perhaps there is a time-warp condition in which there would be no circularity in this reasoning, but it certainly *seems* circular.

* * *

But of course we want to say that it is not only the character of an act *itself* which determines our perception of the act, but also its empirical setting. We want to say that we infer the motives and significance of an act from its context in roughly the way in which we say that we infer the meaning of a word from its context.

Imagine that on a warm day a normally attired man of ordinary appearance knocks on your door, and when you open it, he says, "I love birdseed." How shall we go about interpreting this behavior? If you object that it is impossible to pass judgment on an act pulled out of context in this way, I ask you to remember that nothing can be *out of context*—only *in another context* as all tales of the past must be. But you want to know more about the context. Suppose I add that it is Saturday, July, and high noon . . . does that help? If I continue to add observations of this sort will you have *more* context, a more *complete* context—or only a *different* one? Would it help you to know that he had blue eyes? I can continue to make such observations indefinitely, but surely it is not necessary that you have *all* aspects of the context given, before you can construct a hypothesis to explain his behavior. Indeed, you *could not* have more than a selection of data.

Of course what you want to know is the *relevant* details of the context. But doesn't that assume that there is either a *standard* criterion for relevance or some *particular* way of determining relevance in this case? Relevance is a *transitive* relationship. To what shall my selection of data be relevant?—Obviously to some antecedent hypothesis. But if it is an antecedent hypothesis (this itself is curious for a method *founded* upon observation), where will I get it?

A number of reasonable hypotheses spring to mind. It may be that the man is selling birdseed or that he is your new neighbor with a whimsical turn of mind. (But this latter would demand a non-observable dimension, as would any hypothesis founded upon ironies or contrast with the empirical circumstances.) Or it may be that he likes to eat birdseed, a relatively fat-free food for the subtropical climate, or that he has lost a valued dog named Birdseed (and this comes closest to being a hypothesis-for-all-occasions). Any of several explanations may account for this behavior.

In any case, my hypothesis will dictate my description, and my

hypothesis comes, in turn, out of that amalgam of past experiences and ordering constructs which inform and compose all of
my observations.

You may think that because I emphasize the antecedent
position of hypothesis to description, I radically misunderstand
the nature of hypothesis itself. You may wish to remind me that it
is the nature of a hypothesis to be a preliminary notion which will
be subjected to verification procedures. But I only point to its
prior status in this way to show you that it constitutes a
presumption—albeit a rebuttable one in principle—which has special
emotional, if not epistemological, attraction for organisms who
like (or need) to have their hypotheses *confirmed*, particularly if
they are opposed only by *other people's* hypotheses. Later I shall
discuss the fact that there is no *definitive* procedure or standard
for disverifying a cherished hypothesis, and this combination, I
think, makes the antecedent status of hypothesis to description
important.

But, you will say, enough of this. Let us confine ourselves to
pure description. The man simply uttered an English sentence. For
the rest we must wait until something more solid suggests itself. (If
indeed we *can* restrain ourselves in this way.) Alas, even at this
"safe" descriptive level, I am unsure. What instructs us that "I love
birdseed" is an English sentence rather than a Navajo Indian tonal
invocation. I am trying to remove the temptation to think that
any description can be unalloyed with explanation. And explanation, as I have tried to show, requires more than sense to make
sense of.

* * *

Description has another dimension. Suppose that I come to you
one day and tell you that last night I saw a murder. You may
sympathetically inquire if I was very frightened, but I deny any
fear whatsoever. Is this remarkable? If you ask why, I tell you that
it was because I was in a theater. At this point, if you do not feel
too ill-used, you may inquire what play I saw and I answer that it
was no play at all, or at least that no script was being followed so
far as I could determine. Now you may inquire in what theater
such a production took place and I answer that I am unable to give

it a name we both know. Well, how did I recognize it as a theater? There were curtains on either side of the scene, and the participants in the act were in costume. And if you now see my game, you may inquire whether you are now in costume.

Is this so different from the ordinary way in which we recognize the aspects we select to establish the context of an act? Isn't is absolutely essential that we should perceive analogies and dysanalogies? And it is not yet certain that the context of theater in this case is disallowed. There is always the real murder on stage as when Othello and Desdemona are played by husband and wife, respectively insanely jealous and absolutely innocent. Here our criteria for theatricality falter. I only want to show that there is at least a range of applications of analogy to the interpretation of human behavior. Later I shall argue that the range is unlimited.

The problem of the scope of the contextual frame is analogous to the problem of textual construction faced by literary analysts. You will find persons who advocate interpreting the meaning of a word in a poem in the context of the line in which it appears; in the context of the sentence or stanza; in the context of the whole poem; in the context of other works by the same author; in the context of the literary output of its period; in the context of its geographic or ethnic origins; and in the context of all literary and human experience. Is the notion of context in scientific description less plastic? What are its limits?

* * *

In all of this we have been tacitly assuming that everything we could wish to know about a situation is observable. And to say that it is observable if it exists is merely a definition of existence no less metaphysical than the most orthodox religious definition— "*no* metaphysic" *is* itself a metaphysic.

But we should be careful not to let run rampant our tendency to grant methodological license to behavioral sciences. I am hard pressed to set limits on the category of *response* because it is not only the *significance* of a response which turns, more or less evidently, upon analogy, but even the *presence* of one.

For instance, even if I can distinguish one response from another, which is by no means simple, what shall I count as *no response*? It seems that there is a range of interpretation even here and I can easily imagine cases in which no response is a *definite* response—and is still ambiguous. Imagine a tribe in which the sexes (two) are structurally identical except that the female cannot sing. In all other respects the psychological structure is identical with ours. Here, upon appropriate tests, one might predicate a marriage and might not discover just how bad an index these tests are until it is too late.

The ideal paradigm to demonstrate that science is radically analogical is medicine. The core of medicine is diagnosis. Do we really believe that red spots are a standard commodity for which norms are clearly fixed? My favorite medical diagnostic device (I might say stratagem) is the notion of referred pain. Here we have a tool for all occasions not unlike the psychoanalytic notion of repression or any other conceptual construct in which any sign can be evidence for the presence of *any* condition (as when we say that everyone behaves as he does for selfish motives). What archeological artifact could not be, if we wished it to be, evidence of a high civilization?

Here is an epistemic rock bottom. Not only are the motives of subjects a crucial factor in how we interpret the actions of those subjects, but the question of motive may also be applied with equal force to ourselves, since it is not difficult to see whatever analogies we choose. It is difficult to say whether the instrumentation with which we try to overcome (I could have said camouflage) this plasticity is more deceptive to ourselves or to others, for no matter the power of an electron microscope, it must still be looked through with an eye.

In the judgment of communicative configurations (which and whether), these problems of interpretation are pervasive if you will but examine the permutations of situations we wish to call communicative. And this ought not disturb anyone who does not claim a metaphysical exemption for scientific methods and results (every description is in some sense an explanation) nor should it embarrass anyone who does not suppose that there are natural limits upon the processes of interpretation.

* * *

But perhaps I am again mistaken in my judgment that our

perceptions are suffused with our attitudes. Since we can neither analyze a person without destroying him nor reproduce and synthesize him exactly, I am reluctant to do more than speculate upon the "laws" by which we behave, and my reduction of the edifice of scientific method in communication to analogy is—I need scarcely remind you—only a way of looking at it. I happen to like the attitudes it may promote.

II. *A Philosophic Attitude: The Illusion of the Disappearing judge.*

"Well! I've often seen a cat
without a grin," thought Alice,
"but a grin without a cat! its
the most curious thing I ever
saw in my life!"

—*Alice in Wonderland*

A man is playing poker and his friend, after watching the play for awhile, takes him aside.

Are you so stupid that you can't see that they are cheating you?

I know that they are cheating, but I like to play and theirs is the only game I know of.

Have you looked elsewhere?

No. I am too busy playing.

A wise man was approached by a young man who held a bird in his hands. The young man asked the wise man if the bird was alive or dead.

The bird was alive, but if the wise man answered that it was alive, the young man would crush it to death; if the wise man said that the bird was dead, the young man would release it to fly away.

The wise man said, "The answer my son is in your hands."

In some philosophical circles, the passion for objectivity in *perception* has been replaced by a passion for objectivity in *statement*. Indeed, they are not mutually exclusive and, in some cases, are even complementary—rather like different totalitarian tendencies and, as I shall hope to show you, the analogy doesn't end there. If there is a more pervasive way of coercing us than by illusorily standardizing our perceptions, it is by standardizing (in some ways equally illusorily, because the distinction between analytics and metaphysics is itself illusory) our usage.

The first step in this linguistic uniformity campaign is to attempt the destruction of certain connections between experience and meaning. The ordinary way of doing this is by distinguishing *meaning* from *reference*. The distinction has many variants. One of these is to take different descriptive phrases which refer to a single object (as for instance "morning star" and "evening star" both refer to Venus) and to argue that while their reference is identical, the meanings of the phrases are markedly different; that to destroy the object referred to by these phrases would not be equivalent to destroying the meanings of the phrases. Thus, the reasoning concludes, we can deal with questions of meaning quite apart from the issue of reference.

Another variant of the argument is to argue that certain words seem to have no referents in the non-linguistic world (e.g., "but," "for") and that we do not necessarily learn our language by conjoining words with objects. However, this last is one of those arguments to which I pose the question: which is it that we propose to do, intuit ourselves languageless and record the process by which we learn our language from the inside, or inquire of the languageless in what way they are learning the language? If neither, then we must make behavioral inferences about processes which are unobservable. What is there to say that there is no stage at which terms such as "for" have concrete referents in the minds of learners, which are forgotten with the attainment of greater facility?

The way in which the meaning-reference distinction is argued often makes it seem that questions of meaning, defined in this way, are the only sorts of questions which interest us. Simply put, it may be made to seem that meaning is a closed system and that statements about it are purely descriptive, since these philosophers eliminate by fiat those problems which are associated with relations between language and experience.

I think that these arguments have the effect of making it appear that a straight stick is being bent by its partial submergence in water, when the stick was *already* bent.

Each of these arguments tends to destroy any liaison between the way in which we apply our language to the non-linguistic world and the realm of "pure meaning," which, it is argued, operates on known rules (but known only to some) which one really must observe to be correct.

* * *

I want to argue that rarified air is still air, that the spheres of meaning and experience may be seen as psychologically related, and that, if I am quite wrong on these two points, questions of meaning defined in this way are really unimportant in the partisan activity of language-using.

Synonymity, congruence of meaning, is the hub of meaning. It is our way of showing that a relation durably obtains between two or more linguistic items (e.g., "bachelor" and "unmarried male"). But what is the hub of synonymity? What is the criterion for sameness of meaning between two collocations? One can answer this question in many ways and we want to say that, having chosen, our question of criterion is settled. But suppose that someone disagrees with the posited criterion for sameness or similarity? Such a challenge is invariably followed by the question, usually condescendingly asked, whether it makes any sense to challenge a criterion. Of course it does make sense, but only if there is an application in prospect which will govern interests which are not purely definitional. If there isn't any such application in view, why are we bothering with the question of synonymity?

There is a vacillation in the ordinary case of such proceedings between the privileged definitional status of a chosen criterion (what I shall mean by "same") and the claim, required for persuasive purposes, that the choice is *descriptive* (that it reflects what *others* mean by "same"). But how do we determine the latter? Isn't it by showing that certain criteria for sameness are *used*? But how do we know that a criterion is being used? Isn't it only by making a judgment? And isn't that judgment a judgment of experience? (And let me remind you that this involves applying a principle beyond sense, since we must infer that a collocation is

used *because* of a certain criterion.) *Our description has become
an explanation.*

In any case, even if a criterion for sameness could be selected
"objectively," in its application to pairs of collocations there
would still be a judgment of the presence of sufficient similarity to
meet the criterion. And this rests upon an analogy. I genuinely fail
to see that the sphere of meaning is judgment-free, or even more
judgment-free than that of reference.

Moreover, I fail to see that the two spheres can be separated
psychologically. Why is it that we cannot escape a feeling of
incongruity when an enormous girl is named "Orchid" or when a
toy poodle is named "Prince"?

Let us imagine that we agree on all questions of criteria. Where
are we? Are we necessarily in a better posture to settle questions
of reference? I think not. *Applications* of criteria cannot be settled
simply by stating the criteria. Resolution is only possible by a
further judgment. Later I shall argue that this judgment need not
even be circumscribed within a definite range by criteria. (If this is
so, how important is it to obtain a prescription which can be filled
in any way at all?) Many logicians, correctly anticipating the
abyss, retreat from issues of reference. But surely for the
rhetorician, naming is the name of the game.

* * *

What are the limits of naming? What circumstances or rules
inform and restrict the process of naming? I might, of course, have
said what circumstances or rules *should* inform and restrict the
process of naming? For, as I hope to show you, the question is
inescapably axiological rather than epistemological. The two
ordinary ways of limiting the appropriateness of a name to an
object, circumstance, or situation are context and convention.

I hope already to have done irreparable damage to the notion
that context *necessarily* determines the direction and quality of
our perceptions. And it is but a short jump, without qualitative
hurdles, to the conclusion that external circumstances need not
necessarily limit the ways in which we name our perceptions. If
anything, adding the processes of naming to those of perception
tends to make more indirect our contact with the "objective"
world. Paradoxically, we rely upon verbal reports far more often

than on direct perception to form our judgments of situations. In most cases, verbal reports are the only means available to us whenever we attempt to make judgments on temporally or spatially distant events. And I am inclined here to include film in the category of such second-order reliance, since images on film are limited in many of the same ways as are verbal reports. Point of view is the obvious analog, but one can also find verbal analogs for visual duration, available light, etc., and visual counterparts for voice and mood.

But this is not a radical position in much contemporary philosophy. It is only in science that it's fashionable to think that our linguistic operations need be tied to our perceptions at all. The metaphor which dominates the greater part of the philosophical community just now is the metaphor of language as a self-contained game with definite rules and without any necessary reference to a grid of perceptual or ontological facts. And although many wish to maintain a rigid distinction between our ways of determining meaning and our ways of determining reference, the meaning-model is applied to the processes of naming in the form of reliance upon conventional rules and training to limit the correctness of our application of language to the non-linguistic world. Convention becomes the uninterpretable store of "knowledge."

* * *

Words mean, we are told (and here "mean" is used, at least *in practice*, to govern reference as well), what they *really* mean. But do words *really* mean what they really mean? Is convention an *adequate* determinant of the process of naming and is it an *appropriate* determinant? Here again is the inescapable axiological dimension. And if you find this constant reduction of all questions to the axiological tiresome, I only ask you how we can evaluate alternative roads unless we first know where we want to go?

The view that words will do the work if only we will step aside and let them do it appears in many disguises, ranging from the political-legal fiction that we have a government of laws rather than of men, to the (more primitive?) Fundamentalist "How do I know? The Bible tells me so." But I think that the determination of rules is a complex problem involving an agency *and an actor*. Rules of our language do not appear to us as spirit writing.

Presumably, the rules which are announced by those who write of rules are not pure invention, and, therefore, they must be based upon observation of some sort. In other words, in order to know that a rule is operant you must see it in operation. Indeed you must infer its existence by its observance in use, and this re-establishes the link between meaning and experience.

A rule, then, is not primarily a phenomenon. It is a *construction* and, as such, it is based upon perception and inference, neither of which is necessarily uniform. Since I have already discussed some of the vagaries of observation and report, I shall refrain from rehearsing them here. But the *descriptive* nature of the statement that our use of language is rule-governed, is, in my judgment, questionable, if the process of discovering this fact is to some degree a process, on the part of the observer, of *creating* rules, since this process requires a step beyond sense. If we decide that a rule is being used by observing similarities and variations—and what else is there—then to say that language is rule-governed is to make an observation which is not startling for its penetration, but only for its elegance and its stubbornness. It is, of course, in just this way that we have concluded that *everything* is rule-governed. How convenient. And by rules which we can readily observe. There is, I think, this persistent dilemma. *Our descriptions become either explanations or commands.*

* * *

A much more important and interesting question is: "Who is doing the determining of the conventions of our language?" Who decides which uses of a word are conventional and, therefore, *correct* and which are rule-violating and, therefore, *incorrect*? I remind you that this question may be further subdivided into the determination of what the conventions *are* and the decision on how to *apply* them correctly.

We are now thoroughly trained to expect expert professional decision-making, but we also expect some responsiveness to language as we use it. Modern objectivist linguistic philosophy combines the best devices of collectivism with some devices of the more evident forms of totalitarianism by assuming both popular and expert mantles simultaneously. By this ingenious device, it is made to appear that it is, in fact, *ordinary* language which is being represented (all of us, of course, are *symbolically* present at the deliberations which determine correctness in our speech) and, at the same time, that these important questions are being decided by those who are supremely qualified to make such judgments, and, in this way, to protect us from ourselves. And it is claimed paradoxically that the judgments make themselves. It may or may not be *ordinary* language that is being examined, but the *examination* itself is by no means ordinary, nor is it purely descriptive.

We are forever admonished by these experts to remember our linguistic maladies and to give thanks for the therapy generously provided by professionals. And, getting as much as possible out of the medical metaphor, that resistance to professional treatment is, at worst, sheer perversity in the patient; or, at best, a regrettable lack of discipline.

The notion that reasonable minds may differ is taken to be the worst sort of nineteenth century sentimentality. There are those who take order as the highest *moral* imperative. By this standard, inquiry, lacking proper authorization, is a moral violation and if it threatens to become extended or habitual (one cannot know *in advance* whether an inquiry *must* be infinitely regressive) the transgressor must be silenced, usually by ostracism. We may confidently expect that the next step will be linguistic health units prowling about and ferreting out miscreants and unfortunates to be incarcerated, for the good of all, in institutions for the linguistically insane.

What is the statement, "You *can't* say that," if it is neither the metaphysical statement "This can't occur," nor the causal statement (and thus metaphysical once-removed) "If you do this, this will follow," or "If you do this, this can't follow"? It is a command. I am the first to admit the ubiquity of linguistic muddles, but I would hardly opt for a headache tablet which caused blindness, even if it cured the headache.

Of course it is of the utmost importance to this philosophical program that the *personal* nature of the process be obscured. It must be made to appear that *judgment* has been eliminated and, hence, the need for a judge. I want to take you backstage.

(Please don't be taken in by other strategic distinctions which seem to make themselves automatically; as for instance, the distinction between the cognitive and the non-cognitive, essential and accidental, etc. Obviously, anything you think of is cognitive if we take cognitive to mean simply in your cognition or mentally presented, and if we use a stronger sense of the word then the cognitive/non-cognitive distinction begs the question. Whether a given aspect is cognitive or not is the point at issue. All of these distinctions are disguises for the same illusion.)

* * *

Imagine that you come to my office and I invite you to sit down on a computer. You may be puzzled because, medievally, my office contains nothing which you would ordinarily recognize as a computer. Ever compassionate in the presence of perplexity, I indicate an object and tell you that placing yourself upon it will constitute acceptance of my invitation. What? Is a chair a computer? What prohibits us from saying so? Computers must meet certain criteria. Let us specify them. First a computer must compute. My chair does so by being displaced more or less, and differently, at different moments, by your weight. It must have moving parts. In use, the parts of the chair move in relation to each other and to any fixed point. It must provide a readout of the results of its computations. That is what it does in the differences in its configuration and position after use. It must be electrically powered. And so it is: by the electrical charges of the cells within the muscles of your body. The objectivist linguistic philosopher, if he has succumbed neither to apoplexy nor to his desire to destroy such waywardness, will triumphantly point out to you that the extraordinary use which I have made of the word "computer" had to be *explained* in the ordinary way. But I must ask if that is *necessarily* the case. It need not necessarily be explained to everyone in order that they should grasp my meaning. And, in any case, it is the *product*, the new perspective, which interests me. Wasn't it D. H. Lawrence who said that whatever else the sun may be, it is certainly not a ball of hot gasses?

Now, having a firmly grounded faith in my continued resource-fullness (or what you will), you may wish to object that, with *this kind* of argument, anything could be seen as a computer. Of course. (And don't be disturbed by the logician's trick here; the argument that, in order for the designation to be meaningful, there must be some contrast. I am not arguing that everything *is* a computer, only that this sort of application is not naturally excluded by a set of criteria. Nor am I suggesting that you must accept my curious application; only that you ought to have the *option* of accepting it without the stigma of incorrectness or of intellectual weakness and that criteria do not naturally prohibit you from accepting it *if you wish to*.)

There is inescapably a question of judgment here. I hope that it is clear that the judgment with which we are dealing is of analogy and dysanalogy, and that 'such choices are less trivial (if you insist that this case is trivial) when we are choosing between "assassin" and "executioner," or between "guest" and "trespasser." And isn't there an inescapable dimension of eulogy or dyslogy in whatever name we choose? We are inclined to think of "sexual intercourse" as a neutral way of saying what might be said otherwise—"making love" or "fucking"—but, from one point of view, such a clinical slant upon this phenomenon is equally dyslogistic. And, of course, from another, it seems equally eulogistic. All of these ways of describing an act seem to me hints at explanations which are more or less flattering than other explanations.

* * *

Confronted with such boundary problems, many will invoke the metaphor of the family and suggest that a family relationship obtains among many cases or that the edges of the items of our language are blurred rather than sharp. It should be clear, however, that this is not even a preliminary solution. Rather, it is an obfuscation when we are choosing between two close family members and, in the case of more distant relations, it is obvious that one must draw a limit upon the family—and the limit they want to draw is a conventional one.

But don't we encounter an identical dual problem here to that which we found without the metaphor of the family (and here the analogical reasoning is patent), for we are still without definitive and uninterpretable conventions to make our decisions for us. Expanding a word's use to cover a range doesn't solve the problems of the limits of the range. Any family is infinitely expandable if we wish it so and blurred edges are not edges at all.

Some are inclined to point to the fact that interpretation is not *in fact* an endless process and to call uninterpretable the point at which we stop interpreting. Yet, that point is no more uninterpretable than any other simply because we stop there. Any number of extraneous factors may influence where we actually stop and the crucial question remains, at any given point, *ought* we to continue, since we *may* do so as long as we wish to.

I only want you to see that conventions don't apply themselves; that there is *choice* within the conventions; and that it is *we*, and not the rules, who choose, no matter how we may try to blind ourselves to the fact of choice. Words don't mean what they really mean: they mean what you are persuaded they mean. So I am inclined to say that, in one important sense, things are what you are persuaded they are. If convention is rock bottom, I hope at least to have shown you that it is rock bottoms.

* * *

The problem of limits on the process of naming is still greater if we look beyond familiar realized phenomena to the realm of possible experience. Suppose that when you get into bed tonight your lamp says good night to you. I am not here talking about a radio-lamp, although such items present additional problems of judgment, since we might easily add features indefinitely to the radio-lamp such that it becomes extraordinarily difficult to use hyphenation as a device to postpone judgment. If your lamp commences a conversation with you, is it still properly, *conventionally*, called a lamp?

But you may be inclined to doubt that this will happen. Why is that? Can such an eventuality be dismissed as mere possibility (the really interesting psychological question may be whether we contrast possibility with probability, or with impossibility) and can this possibility be relegated to comparative unimportance? Of course. It is, after all, a question of attitude. But the reasoning behind such an attitude ought to be made plain. One might doubt that that *specific* event will occur, but it is much more likely to encounter doubt that that *kind* of event will occur. And this attitude will be based in the belief that the future will be like the past; put otherwise, that the universe is orderly in ways which we *already* know. And all of this reasoning will melt away into the tacit acceptance of elegance.

You may want to say that, in any case, conventional usage will cover all *ordinary* situations. But then I ask how you will determine if a given situation is ordinary or not. Isn't it by making analogies? And since analogies are not standard commodities, any situation may be regarded as ordinary or not, as you choose. (One is reminded of the poorer mystery fiction of the late 1940s, in which any sequence of events which defied scientific explanation was met with "There's a rational explanation for everything," i.e., all situations are ordinary.)

Although it is a commonplace, I should mention that the assumption of uniformity here is twofold. Not only is there an assumption of perceptual uniformity between the future and the past, but also of linguistic uniformity. And the language changes. Not overnight, you will say. But what indices do you consult? What if you find tomorrow that some of the people you know are using "computer" instead of "chair" in certain situations in which you wouldn't? Has the use of the word "computer" changed? And, if so, is the word being misused, and by whom? For as much as we attempt to lift the onus from *misuse,* it still sounds like a criminal indictment, and this is altogether in keeping with the program of objectivist linguistic philosophy. I suggest that the question, whether or not an extraordinary use is a misuse, is a question of the sort of justification which one generates for that use and how it strikes us. And thus we are again carried inevitably to the level of persuasion.

* * *

One could easily admit the frequently brilliant insights of objectivist linguistic philosophy into the pantheon of perspectives, were it not for the deception—whether practiced upon themselves or upon us I do not know—of objective analysis; which produces the illusion of impartiality and the reality of a linguistic police state governed by wind-up-toy professional philosophers, *sans* free speculation, *sans* holiday, and most frightening of all, *sans* tolerance.

We are in danger of losing all of our respect for individual differences and judgments. And this is like the tragic death of a child, for the whole psychology of individual differences is a comparatively recent phenomenon. Yet convention is only as fixed as our willingness to accept it without question and I think that people may choose to be less conventional than conventions.

When the poet encounters a certain kind of arrangement, he calls it a paradox and he may smile because he is in the presence of a lovely thing. When a logician encounters the same form, he calls it a contradiction and he, too, may smile, but does he smile for the same reason?

If logicians and rhetoricians agree that the use of a particular word for a particular item may be based solely on acceptance and agreement and that the subsequent following of the rule (e.g., red cannot be a verb) is based on agreement only, the logician will call following that rule *logical* or *grammatical* necessity which suggests that the essential necessity is in the logic or grammar. I have been arguing here that any "necessity" is only in the *acceptance* of the logic and that it is not a necessity but only a contingency. Putting it in the former way is coercive. Intersubjectivity is still subject-ivity—not objectivity—and, although it may be sometimes diffi-cult to break a habit, it is not impossible.

* * *

As a corrective, and later as a program, I suggest another attitude. Since language does not apply itself to the non-linguistic world, all attributions of conditions in that world may be seen as projections of individual minds. We are inclined to feel the need for an indirect object of the attribute "good," i.e., to ask, "Good for whom or what?" Why shouldn't all judgments be taken as transitive in this way? It is easy to see that we don't use the terms "high," "lucky," or "ugly" without some indirect object. But we are quick to do so for "logical," "true," and "responsible." But don't we need to specify, in these cases as well, a judging mind? This attitude seems eminently reasonable in the use of some adjectives (judgments of quality, etc.) and it could be extended to cover acts and objects as well. Even ordinary acts and objects may be regarded as projections of particular minds, and judgments may differ. And if it is argued that a given *statement* may be true or logical by virtue of conforming to a system (I think that this is the less interesting sort of truth and that it still requires a judgment), surely *acts* need not be so formulated, and an important function of statements is to report acts for judgment. (Is it murder or self defense, party or orgy?)

I think that when we say that a statement or an argument *makes sense*, an important dimension of that sense is individual. Words are indicators only to individual minds, and to think of judgment without judges ,may be both elision and illusion. Consider this exchange from *Through the Looking Glass*:

> "There's glory for you!"
>
> "I don't know what you mean by 'glory,' " Alice said.
>
> Humpty Dumpty smiled contemptuously. "Of course you don't—till I tell you. I meant 'there's a nice knock-down argument for you!' "
>
> "But 'glory' doesn't mean 'a nice knock-down argument,' " Alice objected.
>
> "When I use a word," Humpty Dumpty said, in rather a scornful tone, "it means just what I choose it to mean—neither more nor less."
>
> "The question is," said Alice, "whether you *can* make words mean so many different things."
>
> "The question is," said Humpty Dumpty, "Which is to be master—that's all."

I am certainly not prepared to endorse Humpty Dumpty's *tone*, but, as to his conclusion, I am inclined either to agree that the question is indeed which is to be master (if we are flexible enough to take it that there is a question of mastery at all) or to say that the real question is the *manner* in which we master our words. For what is wrong with Humpty Dumpty's definition of the word "glory"? Is it *wrong* exactly? At best, his attitude toward usage is unconventional, and at *worst*, it is chaotic, but I insist that his attitude deserves the status of a position, preliminarily at least.

I suggest that it is not the definition which Humpty Dumpty gives of the word which gives us pause, but rather the apparent absence of any justification for the definition. In its present form, Humpty Dumpty's use of the word "glory" is perhaps unconvincing.

But suppose that instead of adopting the classic attitude and tone of the tyrant, Humpty Dumpty had retorted to Alice's (no less pedantic) objection that glory *doesn't mean* a nice knock-down argument, that it is most often a flag or emblem which reminds us of glory (one country even calls its flag *Old Glory*) and that the flying of a flag over some territory or other is almost invariably the result of a knock-down argument (this is perhaps an understatement) and that by *nice* he means *particular* or *fussy* (which territorial arguments so seldom are these days).

And yet perhaps Humpty Dumpty was doing Alice a kindness in allowing her to supply her own justification for the use of the word, since that posture allows for justification in the interpreting mind and forces it to exercise itself, despite the fact that she chose not to exercise her imagination.

Looked at in this way, definition is a rhetorical resource from *both* sides of a configuration and may be justified in a variety of unconventional ways. Surely the question is open to judgment. I grant that this is a perverse view of communication by current standards and later it will grow perverser still. In any case, it is we who decide questions of reasonableness—not words themselves. Words may be wearing masks far more varied than those which occur to the locked and orderly mind.

All that I have said so far is only to show you that science and logic are only ways of looking, rooted in metaphors. And when I say that these ways of looking are only the spinning-out of metaphors, I do not mean *merely* metaphors as opposed to some other *sort* of thing. I have simply tried to show that if you *like* another way of looking, there is nothing to constrain you except a metaphor. I am neither derogating metaphors nor standing above them. I have only a metaphor to offer.

III. *Four Elementary Propositions Toward a Rhetorical View of Language-Using.*

You who are a fairly reasonable
man, you should have noticed
that nothing in the world is
natural; nothing at all.

What is it that is orange, hangs from the ceiling, and whistles?

I don't know.

A horse.

Why is it orange?

Because I painted it orange.

Why does it hang from the ceiling?

Because I hung it there.

Why does it whistle?

I don't know.

If a wizard offers a man infinite extension of all of his senses, the man may refuse—because he would lose the most precious sense of all.

We speak of poetic or artistic license as the sum of the dispensations necessary to an artistic perspective on the use of language and I hope to have shown you that scientific and philosophical license are necessary to arrive at their linguistic perspectives. Now I want to offer four propositions to element a rhetorical view of language-using which, taken together, may be seen as constituting rhetorical license, and which result in the posture which I shall call radical strategism (which is itself strategic, a strategy of excluding exclusions).

Like the elementary propositions of other perspectives, these are propositions of policy rather than of fact; and propositions of policy are not grounded in observation, but rather in values. Thus, policies may be seen as actuated attitudes. The priority of values appears to be essential in both constructing and in interpreting a theoretical framework, for we cannot choose a path before we know where it is we wish to go and, having decided upon a terminus, it is mere technology to make the road's traversal practical. In this sense, it is better to know *why* and not *how* than it is to know *how* and not *why*.

I have referred to various dualist stratagems which are designed for the purpose of dismissing from intellectual consideration certain aspects of phenomena (relevant/irrelevant, essential/acci-dental, cognitive/non-cognitive, and the like) but I have reserved for final consideration the dualist stratagem which is used to dismiss from *primary* intellectual consideration perhaps more insights and questions than all of the others combined, i. e., to relegate them to a systematic position of secondary importance. It is the separation of the literal and the metaphoric. I will offer an antidote to this separation in the form of four propositions. Radical strategism, then, may be seen as that perspective in which elimination—and, ultimately, the decision process itself—is eliminated.

1. *The substance and forms of argument may be seen as analogy-based*.

Imagine that I witness a murder and that, later, you ask me how I felt at the time. I may be uncertain as to how to know *myself* how I felt and I may lack the means, power, or control of expression to tell *you* how I felt. Both problems are complex, and the fact that they can be separated tells us that communication, as we ordinarily think of it, *need* not be involved unless we wish it to be.

In order to know how I felt in a particular situation, or how I feel in an immediate one (it is not at all essential that the situation should be past, for I am not concerned with *remembering* how I felt—we can assume that some form of sense-memory is present—but with *identifying* it in order to be able to understand it in relation to other possible or actual states) I must have some criteria for different kinds of feelings. This is necessary for purposes of argument (and I do not *necessarily* mean for argument with someone else), regardless of whether I had criteria *before* I had the feelings or not. This last is, for rhetoric, a more or less empty, introspective question. The rhetorical fact is that, in order to generate discourse in such matters, it is essential that I find known points of reference. (I shall use the terms "definitions," "criteria," and "limits" more or less interchangeably to designate these points of reference.)

Generally speaking, we tend to look for these points of reference in two linguistic loci. I do not mean to imply that language is the sole repository of knowledge about experience, or that it is identical with experience, or that it is a complete index of experience. Each of these propositions is closed to intersubjective investigation. I only suggest that we seem to generate two sorts of descriptions of our experiences for ourselves, as well as for others. We tend to use adjectival terms and, when we are questioned by ourselves or others as to their vagueness, we attempt some more precise description. But how to make more precise one's general qualitative experiences? Isn't there only one way; by situationalizing them? That is, by finding analogous and dysanalogous experiences with which to compare instant cases. Eventually, we begin to explore what a particular experience is *like*. And this tendency results in a good deal of bad prose and absurd medical diagnosis, as well as some useful insights. In short, we are led by analogies.

The analogous experience to which I have reference need be within *your* experience only if communication, in the ordinary sense, is important in the particular instance; i.e., only if it is your question and not my own that I seek to answer.

I omit consideration of precise and detailed physiological descriptions of our experiences, insofar as such descriptions are possible, although they would not be ruled out for some specially trained persons. Nevertheless, I hope to have shown you earlier that these, too, are analogy-based.

Isn't it this method to which we normally have recourse when questions occur, and isn't this the means of identifying our experiences for the purpose of understanding and subsequently manipulating them?

Many people want to say that analogies mislead us. But this only confirms that they do, in some sense, lead us. And how can analogies be said to mislead us, unless we *already* know the correct answers—and how did we establish them?

From the discussion thus far, it may appear that the making of analogies is the *last* alternative in a complex process to which we consciously repair only in cases of severe difficulty. On the contrary, I shall argue that all liaison between our language and experience may be seen as analogy-based. We are used to thinking of metaphor and analogy as *means* or vehicles for telling us what a thing is by telling us what it is *like* (as we are used to thinking that there are alternative modes of being and likeness). I shall argue that we ought to think of metaphor and analogy as *ends*, and that there may *be* only like and unlike.

Remember that the universe of discourse which interests us is argument, though not necessarily argument with another person. I shall urge later that this ought to be taken to represent no less than the total linguistic universe, but here let us suppose that I am merely recording my determination to see given collocations as arguments, rather than as expressions, descriptions, ejaculations, or what you will.

Arguments are made of words and other things, the inclusion of which is justified by words, and in many cases which interest us, they are made of proposed liaisons between linguistic items and some aspect of the non-linguistic world. Where such liaisons are proposed (roughly where an act of naming occurs) the argument perspective prompts us to ask for some justification for the liaison. I want to explore the paths of that justification.

* * *

The determination to require justifications for names—that orientation which sees words as partisan names rather than pieces in a self-contained analytic system—is part of what differentiates rhetoric from certain current schools of philosophy. The only alternative to offering some sort of rhetorical justification in response to a question concerning the application of a particular word in a given case is to take the position that no justification need exist for any act of language-using, or that the only possible justification resides in the correct application of an extant convention. And the shift of focus from justification for purposes of argument to the existence of prior justification for the use of a word is part of what differentiates the philosophical from the rhetorical perspective. So that, even if it makes no philosophical sense to some people to seek other-than-conventional justification for our linguistic behavior, it always makes rhetorical sense to do so. In this respect, then, philosophy and rhetoric explore different universes.

I am reluctant to say that one explores more practical ground than the other, because one never knows *beforehand* what sort of exploration will be practical in particular cases. A defense attorney might look for a *reasonable* justification for an act of a defendant, but *unreason* may also be a defense. One can use philosophy to rhetorical ends, and the rhetorician might very well take the philosophical position that our acts are reasonless if he were using that position for a rhetorical purpose. And, although in most cases attorneys are pleading that different words should be applied to a particular act (e.g., "accident" instead of "murder"), in some cases all that one need demonstrate is that the justification for the other name is lacking.

Nor can I see a radical difference in the ultimate ground for rhetorical and philosophical perspectives. It is easy to see that the sorts of investigations required to explore many philosophical questions are largely introspective, but, despite the claims of the scientifically oriented rhetorician, I hope to have demonstrated that questions about the effect of the use of language upon others, resting as they do upon causal inferences, demand no less personal commitment and thus produce only satisfaction, not proof.

But I think that it is fair to say that a radical difference lies in the *disposition* of philosophy and rhetoric. I find the locus of the difference between some philosophers and some rhetoricians not in a different epistemology, but in a different axiology, and I find the question of justification for language-using to be not so much a question of *fact* as a question of *value*. The issue then becomes not "Is there a reason beyond convention to name as we do?" but "Ought we to look for reasons beyond convention to name as we do?" To which question the philosopher may answer, "Not necessarily." But, for the rhetorician, unless he is serving a particular partisan interest of unreason or is on holiday, the one thing which he may not do is refuse to question.

* * *

Arguments are made, in one sense, of words and, in order to show that argument is analogy-based, I must show that an act of naming, for purposes of argument, is analogy-based. Suppose that, one day as we are strolling together, you point to a nearby person and ask me whether or not it is Stanley, who is familiar to both of us. Imagine that you recognize this person as Stanley and that I do not. How will you convince me that it is he? You may call my attention to various features or attributes of this person which indicate that he is Stanley. You may point out to me the white spider web-like hair, the dust-grey, slow eyes, the bulbous nose, the stooped posture, and the well . . . the unpleasant feet. But I deny that it is Stanley, either by attending to other features or by not seeing the ones you see (or smell) as you see them. How are we arguing, and about what?

You are giving criteria and I may either assent to these and distinguish the present case, or offer other criteria; that is, we may argue about the *constitution* of the definition of Stanley or about the manner in which the definition is *applied* to an instant case. Arguments of the former type are often called semantic arguments and may be resolved in various ways; by allowing an authority to intervene, by compromise, etc. In any case, it appears that there is no alternative to generating criteria, however many and however they may be chosen. (In the present case, it would be no less an employment of criteria if we went up to the person and touched him or listened to his voice or, indeed, asked his name.) But, n.b., the decision will always be between *partial* lists of criteria.

But how do we proceed with the argument if we agree upon the criteria to be employed, but disagree on the applicability of those criteria in this case? It is apparent that our disagreement is one of judgment, but judgment of what? Is it not inescapable that we are judging likeness and unlikeness, regardless of our intention to use argument from analogy? It seems that the process is inherent for these purposes since the only alternative, an unsupported assertion that such-and-such is the case, is unacceptable in the context of argument.

Such judgments have two usual forms. They may take the form, as in the present case, that an immediate phenomenon or one recalled from past experience does or does not fulfill a certain definition. Although it may not seem at once that such judgments are of matters of analogy, we can easily show that they are. Imagine that instead of a verbal description or definition, or a mental image against which to measure the present case, we projected an external image of Stanley as we last saw him. The use of this device makes two things clear: that we are comparing an immediate case with a prototype, which we can now see is a judgment of likeness, and that the judgment is indeed one of likeness rather than of identity—for, surely, Stanley will have changed over the years (or even days or hours, although we may have to look more carefully to notice the more or less gradual changes wrought by hours) since we last saw him.

Where the application of a name to a non-linguistic phenomenon is at issue, the other form which judgment customarily takes is more easily recognized as a judgment of similarity. Particular cases, in order to qualify for a particular name, must fall within a certain range by possessing certain attributes, e.g., a table must have an upper surface. Since the criteria will not apply themselves, we must judge whether the case meets them, i.e., whether this object has an upper surface or not. Argument on this point may take the form of comparing the object in question, not with a prototype, but with other cases acknowledged to belong or not to belong to the class to which the case at issue bears resemblances.

Thus, when we argue that an object *is* a table by virtue of having this or that attribute or set of attributes, the substance of the argument may be that it is sufficiently *similar*, but not identical, to other tables to merit the name. In what way does this argument for a *literal* name differ from the form contained in what we usually call a *metaphor*, which asserts a partial resemblance of two entities? I do not think that they need be seen as arguments of different kinds. If you want to say that the distinction may be in the degree of similarity required, I ask just where the boundaries lie.

Nothing is identical to anything else in all respects and in exact degree and using a name does not imply identity with other objects in a class. Nor is anything totally, absolutely, and objectively dissimilar to anything else. That which two things have in common may be that they both differ from a norm, even if they are in some sense opposite, e.g., high and low blood pressure.

The difference between literal statement and metaphor may be just in the limits to which we are willing to stretch our linguistic and conceptual categories.

A distinction should of course be made between literal statement versus metaphor and the linguist's distinction between "nuclear" and "marginal" uses, in which frequency of occurrence is used as sole determinant.

I suspect that, in use, the word "literally" is only a way of adding emphasis and, if it is not, it ought to be, for where it is used to enshrine certain perspectives, I ask whether we have a uniform way to grade similarities and differences.

Looking at language-using in this way allows us to say that any use of a word may be seen as equally literal or metaphoric with any other use, and to abandon the dualistic perspective of two *kinds* of language, one discursive (scientific) and one presentational (poetic), with which we are usually encumbered, and by which vast areas of intellectual activity are assigned to art, as contrasted (usually invidiously) with science (to *know*). I genuinely fail to see that Aristotle's spinning out of the metaphor of Entelechy or Plato's of the metaphor of Eros are less properly called "knowledge" than is the careful observation of Professor Pavlov's dogs.

This way of looking at language-using provides the foundation for a rhetorical perspective, the beginning of which is the automatic transformation of *being* into *likeness*, the substitution of "as" for "is" in statements, and, in our thinking, the addition of the more complete form "may be seen as" to all identifications. Since all naming may be seen as identification, all descriptive statements are transformed by this perspective into statements of analogy.

* * *

Of course this will develop into sheer Sophistry—and Sophistry, in the sense of argument for the sake of argument, is what I shall advocate. But I think that this need not be construed to mean argument to deceive others, because that would imply that we *already* know the truth. Nor need it mean argument to make the worse appear the better reason, because that would imply that we know which is which *beforehand*.

This adjustment of focus from identity to analogy is a linguistic approach to the reinstatement of a perspective which was discarded when the law of identity (and its fellows, non-contradiction and the excluded middle) became the second law of reason. (The first law was that the second law took precedence over all others.) We forget that the law of identity itself may be read as an injunction to accept an analogy, to take a thing *as* itself rather than *as* something else. And we are at such pains to avoid the opprobrium associated with the *practice* of Sophistry (usually taken as playing about the superficial) that we forget the utility of the sophistic *insight* that it is *we* who determine the matter and form of identity. I remind you that the opprobrium associated with Sophistry is only slightly greater than that associated with rhetoric itself. Our inclination has been to attempt to escape this abuse by attempting to equate rhetoric with science or with logic, or with both, rather than to defend, or perhaps even to urge, a genuinely rhetorical viewpoint.

The soul of this radically analogical viewpoint—as opposed to its mind—is that there should be no exemptions to its injunction to tentativeness, no special-status truths allowed. (This clearly dispenses with sanctions against contradiction.) And this may seem to render it self-defeating for, inasmuch as its restraint would apply equally to the analogical perspective itself, the possibility of literalism would be readmitted. Of course. And aside from the strategic admonition not to take literalism literally which I have already urged, the only defense for the integrity of the analogical perspective is in its value. But this should surprise no one who didn't think that the ground for the perspective was otherwise. If it had been analytic, the objection that one must have at least a single case of literalness to contrast with the metaphoric perspective might have some point. I shall address this objection more fully later, but I want to say here that, in a way, this objection begs the question by *assuming* the "is" perspective. I have not been saying that "is" *is* "as", but only that it *ought* to be taken as "as"—It grows curioser and curioser.

If you are impatient you now want to say, "So what if we do, where will it lead us?" And I can only tell you where I hope it might lead; from a metaphor (all metaphor itself), through a set of attitudes, to a set of policies embodying some terminal values, which I reserve the right to withhold until the end. Isn't that where terminal values belong?

* * *

Arguments are made of sentences arranged in certain ways, and I propose to show that analogical reasoning may be found at the core of *all* of the forms which we call rational inductive arguments. The foundations of deduction are in question and, although there are schools of thought which hold that deduction is derived from experience, I do not include deduction in this discussion.

The variety of patterns of inductive argument may be taken to be derivative of two basic forms; argument from generalization and argument from cause (e.g., sign arguments seem to be derived from a basic causal pattern). I want to hold that generalizations and causal arguments may be seen as derivative of analogy, and that analogy is the most *fundamental* and *primitive* form of reasoning, in that it must precede the other forms. I remind you that I am not here speaking of analogy as a *psychological* mechanism, entity, or process which is implicit in thinking, but of analogy as the adhesive of *argument*, so that whether or not we compare for ordinary verification, we do where persuasion of ourselves or others is involved.

Consider the argument that a particular earthquake caused damage to a certain building. In order to establish the causal relationship, we must show that the earthquake possessed the potency and immediacy to have produced the damage. But how do we establish that the earthquake was sufficiently potent? Is it not by consulting our experience with earthquakes of a certain range of magnitude and with buildings of a certain range of types; and how do we establish that the present earthquake and the present building fall within those ranges, if not by analogy?

Similarly, if we wish to establish the point at issue as a generalization (argument is a form, not a set of facts, and various forms may be applied to the same facts), we have the task of showing that a present instance falls within the range covered by the appropriate probability charts; and how shall we do so, where there is an issue, but by analogy (e.g., the process of likening this building to others in the range by material, plan, etc.)?

This is really no more than to say that the stuff of inductive argument is *example,* and that the process of *selecting* and *handling* examples for purpose of argument is radically analogy-based. What else would instruct us in the gathering and classification of examples? Causal arguments bear the additional burden of establishing similarities between relations of events, again instructed or projected by analogy alone.

But is analogy an inductive argument at all? Is it derived from our experience or does some integrative process govern the range of those experiences, such that we predetermine that range, unwittingly or otherwise? I do not know, and I cannot think by what process I might find out. I have only been concerned to show that, whatever its origin and constitution, analogy is both the structural and the substantive adhesive of argument.

    2. *Analogies may be seen as possessing equal truth-value.*

    But of course it is Stanley: the same eyes, the same ironical twist to the mouth, the same nicotined index finger. Who else could it be? (Of course you do not intend this as a serious question; by what method would we attempt to discern who else it *could* be?) I *am* sorry, but I still do not see that it is Stanley. What do I mean? Do I mean that I agree that all of these attributes combined signify Stanley, but that I do not find them as you do? Or do I mean that the sum of these observations falls short of convincing me, though I agree with each of them? We know where the former road will lead, but suppose now that we take the latter. Suppose that I say that your listing of Stanley's traits is not sufficiently comprehensive to conclude that we have the man here. If you ask how many analogous properties will persuade me, are you really asking for a *number*? If so, what will you regard as a *reasonable* number? Surely the process of *simply* numbering similarities, and dissimilarities must end in a tie or in the inevitable result of a contest of resistance to fatigue, which is no decision at all.

    Let us suppose that we pursue this path for awhile, just to satisfy our curiosity about its byways. At one point, while listing dissimilarities, I mention that our present object of discussion is not wearing any of the suits which Stanley used to possess. We are both acquainted with Stanley's wardrobe. Here you may stop me. Am I serious? Can I be arguing that we may take anything so *accidental* as a suit as a criterion of identity, or, as we now say, similarity with our model? Why not? I may hold that the very essence of Stanley is his suit. But you have been attending to attributes such as the color and shape of the eyes of our two cases (the instant and the model), and you must point out that these ought to be preferred as criteria, since one cannot change one's eyes as quickly or easily as one can one's clothes. (If you say this, you have not spent nights like some of the nights I have spent; and of course, technology makes all things possible.)

    Very well, I am not unreasonable, despite contrary claims by those who already know all the forms of reasonableness. Let us agree on that single attribute (the eyes) as essential in our judgment. Now, after I attend to them carefully, I say that they are not Stanley's eyes at all. If we list further properties of Stanley's eyes, we may disagree on *their* application—on the manner in which we project the model onto the present case—so let us spare ourselves that trial.

But beyond that question, what are we arguing about? In one sense, we are speaking of physical properties, but, in another, we are speaking of a non-physical entity: *Similarity*. But what does similar mean? Or, to put it in our present frame, what is the criterion for similarity itself? I confess that I do not know, and, if you do, I shall look forward to your letter. Lacking this criterion, how can we evaluate and hierarchize the process of analogy? Note that I am not only pointing out our lack of a criterion for similarity as an *abstract* property (and of what is it a property, objects or comparing minds?), but in conjunction with *specific physical attributes,* or even with particular *aspects* of those attributes. By what criterion do we judge whether the shapes of two sets of eyes are similar? How much difference constitutes dissimilarity? If nothing that I have called a matter of judgment before seemed a matter of judgment to you, I hope that you will assent to the proposition that the question of the presence or absence of similarity is a question of judgment, i.e., one for which we lack precise norms and measures. I remind you that the classical way of distinguishing metaphoric from literal analogy is the similarity of the analogized pair.

Again, even if we agree upon some measures of similarity (what would such measures be like?) our criteria would still not *apply themselves* to particular cases. Whether we are dealing with similarity itself, or with degrees of similarity between two cases, or with the presence or absence of a particular object, our criteria, whatever they may be, must still be projected onto particular instances, and there is an infinite number of ways to do this. Is there any object that is not computer-like if we wish it to be? Since no criterion *naturally* excludes any application of itself, analogies do not have *natural* limits, and *imposed* limits will only be as imposing as their justifications. And if language-using is radically analogy-based, this lack of limits is a pervasive phenomenon.

If you insist on what are called *reasonable* examples, consider these. Imagine that we have a divine injunction against killing other human beings, except in self-defense or in defense of the lives of others. Imagine that our highest courts hold that this threat to life must be immediate. What, beyond judgment, prohibits the mass execution (another interestingly plastic notion) of the people in concentration camps or industrial cities during World War II from qualifying as self-defense, even given our criteria? Is not an (alleged) economic threat, or an (alleged) industrial threat considered immediate? If you are appalled by this reasoning, remember that it seems to have persuaded somebody; and that the only antidote may be another argument.

Or, how do we distinguish *naturally* between acts of courage and acts of compulsion, in order that we may assign human merit appropriately? And we will find the Roman Catholic Pope's infallibility on matters of faith and morals formidable indeed, if we ask ourselves what sorts of matters *cannot* be so construed.

If you really think that we have a government of laws rather than of men I shall let you *write* the laws while I merely *apply* them. I do not say that one need *necessarily* see analogy, and thus naming, as plastic. But seeing it that way is indispensable to a rhetorical attitude. Where to end the extension of extension is a matter of judgment.

Can we *set* limits? In one sense, yes (we can agree upon criteria) but, in another sense, we cannot limit the ways in which criteria *may* be applied, except by authority (which may also be difficult) or by persuasion. And I do not mean to imply that these two are necessarily distinct, or that one cannot always be seen as a form of the other.

* * *

Seeing language-using in this way puts several traditional notions in question. For if there is not an objective way to number or extend analogies, or aspects of analogies, not only are concepts of good and bad or better and worse inappropriately regarded as properties of phenomena, but rather as judgments of individuals, but several other standards and categories of language-using are affected. Descriptions, definitions, or any application of language to a non-verbal entity—or even to another verbal one—are no longer regarded as differentially *correct*, but rather as differen- tially *persuasive*. Ostensive definitions or examples, or any application of the non-verbal world to the verbal, are no longer seen as differentially *correct*, but rather as differentially *persua- sive*. In short, language-using is de-objectified and de-absolutized.

Indeed the categories true and false, as applied to statements are rendered radically subjective, for, since the truth-value of an empirical proposition rests upon naming some non-verbal entity, and names, in turn, rest upon analogy—which may be as plastic as we wish—any empirical statement may be taken as true or false, in the sense that words may or may not be applied in a particular way if we wish. Thus, any description of a phenomenon could be a correct description and it would add little to label the descriptive sentence "true" for the emphasis would always be on *true by virtue of persuasion* which implies a judging mind.

If we adopt this perspective, yet another categorical distinction of traditional logic loses its limits in use. In logical parlance, the *denotation* of a word is its extension, the objects or entities to which it applies, i.e., those objects or entities which possess the properties which entitle them to the name. Clearly, the limits on that class of objects or entities for any word disappear if we regard naming as analogy-based and analogy itself as limited only by lack of convincing justification which, again, I need scarcely remind you, is a matter of *individual judgment.*

I know of no way to predict the ways in which these judgments may be achieved or influenced. It may be a matter of determination alone. If it is the case that inside every argument there is an analogy, it may be that inside every analogy is an act of sheer will. That will, in combination with linguistic and perceptual plasticity, may account for the phenomenon of dreams foretelling future events and is, of course, the fortune teller's reliable aid. And I think that it may account no less fully for the edifice of accredited knowledge.

*　*　*

It will be objected, no doubt, that such a way of accounting for knowledge makes of the sense-world, and the conceptual frame thereof, a giant thematic apperception test. I do not wish to escape this charge. I wish to urge it, for it is the *generative* power of language which I think ought to be of paramount rhetorical interest. The scientific and objectivist philosophical perspectives try to chain the Prometheus of language and I think that it is the task of the rhetorical perspective to free language from these chains. I hope that this way of putting it will answer the charge of negativeness in my approaches to the scientific and philosophical perspective. I am simply attempting to negate their negations, and that constitutes an affirmation. It is an affirmation of the power of language used by individual minds to dissent from and to re-form, as well as to form community. It is only the community aspects of language that are recognized by science and objectivist philosophy, at the expense of the generative powers.

The rhetorical perspective is not without its cost. To court the generative powers of language is to lose the comfortable conviction that we already have all of the possible answers when we ask a question, and this increases, the ambit of other risks. Either way, there is a price to pay. You must decide which is the higher.

If God submitted the act of creating the universe for appropriate placement in the cosmic structure of disciplines, there would be advocates to argue that it was an endeavor in physics and others who would argue that it was an endeavor in engineering. I would attempt to make a case for rhetoric. He created it by naming names.

3. *Language-using may be seen as radically strategic.*

I have argued that language-using seen from a rhetorical perspective is an act of choice, and that this alone is sufficient to render it radically strategic. But it is not only the fact of choice which demonstrates the strategic dimension in language-using, but also the radically *partial* product of the choice. I hope to demonstrate that the partiality obtains both in the sense of *incomplete* and also in the sense of *biased*.

Strategic implies adversaries on a battlefield, as well as a choice of tactics, and we may visualize the linguistic battlefield in various ways, depending on whether we emphasize the agent or the agency. In my view, it would add nothing to say that language *itself* is strategic, since it may be argued that language, as a living phenomenon, does not come into being until we use it, and that, even if we visualize it as active, it is *human beings* who determined its constitution initially. Besides, it would be painfully obvious to you at this point that I am again urging the axiological position that language *ought* to be seen as strategic. Therefore, I choose to speak in terms of language-*using*.

If I can show you that the ordinary processes of description and definition may be seen as partial in use, the ubiquity of these processes, will, I think, demonstrate the fundamentally strategic quality of language-using. I hope to have already shown you that we are not objective in our ways of dealing with perceptual data, but I want to call your attention now to a consequence of that lack of objectivity. And here, of course, I am not referring to a state of mind, but to the fact that choices of aspects of perceptual situations other than those to which we give careful attention, are both *possible* and *reasonable*.

* * *

Suppose that I ask you to synopsize the events of Shakespeare's *Othello*. In order to characterize an act, you must, to some extent, characterize an actor. How do you perceive the title character? Do you attend to his profession or to his racial background or to his powers in the play or to some other attribute or relation? Surely, your perception of Othello will be in some way *apportioned*, i.e., you will not attend to *all* of his attributes *equally*, nor will you attend to them simultaneously and, thus, there will be, in your perception, at least a *temporal* hierarchy the impact of which we can only guess.

I only want to call your attention to this in order to show you that there will be some *efficiency* in your perceptions, in the sense that you will tend to highlight some aspects of the character, and also to show you the important axiomatic consequence that, in so doing, you will have to *suppress* other aspects. It is a common-place that perception is, in some ways, structured. I only want to remind you that what you *omit* to do is part of what you *do*.

But I think that there is a second process to consider. Or, at least, it may be seen as a separate process, whether or not it is part of the perceptual process psychologically. I want to show that, for rhetorical purposes, there may be two sets of choices to make and that, if we attend to them as separate sets, we may vastly increase our rhetorical resources.

* * *

What will you enter opposite *Othello* in the *dramatis personae*? (Roughly, what definition or description will you give? For here, description and definition come perilously close to merger.) It may seem that, once having chosen an aspect or aspects of

Othello's character to which to attend, descriptions follow by some logical or conventional process. But there are still choices. Suppose that you select Othello's race as an essential aspect of his character. You may describe him as "black," "negro," "Moor," etc. Suppose that you choose his status in the play. You-may describe him as "husband," "lover," "foil," etc. Suppose that you choose his profession. You may describe him as "soldier," "governor," "warrior," etc. We do not have only one naturally correct description for each phenomenon, or vice versa—no matter how much that state of things may be desired by the post office-minded—and I need scarcely remind you that to exhaust all of the possibilities could be an endless process.

If so many choices are possible for the description of a single character, imagine the range of choices in describing an act involving characters, relations and qualities. Imagine what could be involved in describing a *pas de deux* at any given stage of the dance. There are choices of active and passive partner, possession, relative motion, degrees of completion, etc. And is it not so for all language-using involving the relation of words to non-verbal entities or states?

Consider the ease with which we may alter our perspectives on quality with minimal transposition in our descriptions. There seems a gulf between describing a person as "capable of not loving," and "incapable of loving" (or as "incapable of being influenced," and as "capable of being uninfluenced"). And what invitation to our admiration, or to our inducement, in "poor but honest" and "honest but poor"?

* * *

But, n.b., when I say that language-using is strategic, I mean neither that it need be so *intended*, nor that it does, *in fact*, produce any particular effect upon others. I mean only that it allows choice among alternative ways of saying, and that each *could* introduce a different perspective. And as to whether two ways of describing assert the same fact, this question turns at least upon some criteria for *same*, and so it may be as we wish. It is a question of attitude.

Nor need we see the process of giving definitions, even taken as the process of setting up purely analytic relations, as less strategic. A definition says less or more than might be said, and thereby implies choice and partiality.

Moreover, I do not see that descriptions should be regarded as *differentially* reductive, for I cannot conceive how we would establish a *quantification* of a given description's omissions. And of course I include the above description of description. Every description may be taken as equally reductive, and every proposition as equally strategic. And thus my description of an object as a computer is no more strategic than to call it a chair.

Although we may now be disinclined to call what is merely conventional *neutral* or *objective*, we may still be inclined to mistake scientific descriptions for neutral ones. From a rhetorical viewpoint, however, it is no more or less objective, nor more or less reductive, to call an act "sexual intercourse," than it is to call it "making love" or to call it "fucking."

Thus, I add to the admonition to see *is* as *as*, the admonition to see each *as* as a selection among equally reductive alternatives. To the extent that language-using describes, it reduces. And to the extent that it reduces, it recommends a way of looking at something. Thus, language-using may be seen as a radically strategic act.

* * *

Let me attempt to disarm some methodological objections which I have hinted at before. The analytically inclined (not as contrasted with the superficially inclined but with the experimentally inclined) will want to call my attention to a grievous error in my theoretical formulations. I have said that all language-using is partial; definitions, because they highlight some aspects of a *class*, and omit or suppress others, and descriptions, because they operate similarly upon *phenomena*. And it seems that I have used the term "partial" without an opposite, thus robbing it of sense. If no language-use is complete then the term "partial," many will argue, has no meaning as applied to language-use.

In one sense, this is a formal requirement, and I can answer by saying that the term "complete" has a use, but is incorrectly applied to the processes of perception, definition, and description. I may then argue either that it may be correctly applied to other phenomena (such as emotions or ontological objects) or that the term has a *use*, which is its meaning, but that the class of *complete* entities is empty, as the more sophisticated empiricists do with the term "metaphysical". Either of these ways of doing will satisfy the formal analytic objection that the term is being used without an opposite.

But there remains the *substantial* objection that to have sense, a term must have an opposite. I think that there is an analytic defense to this objection, for implicit in the demand for an opposite is an absolute, i.e., that language must be used dialectically.

The dilemma is this: to say that a word must derive meaning from an opposite is equivalent to saying that words mean only dialectically. But then "dialectical," as applied to the meaning of words, has no opposite, i.e., we would need a non-dialectical way of doing in order to respect the dialectical rule as applied to the term "dialectical". And one would have to say that, in order for it to make sense to use a word *with* an opposite, it would have to make sense to use a word *without* an opposite. Otherwise, the rule would be self-contradictory.

But if, in order to prevent the rule from contradicting itself, we exempt "dialectical" from the dialectical requirement, why should not other exemptions also be granted, for other good reasons? The rule is either self-contradictory or ineffective, and we may do as we wish.

But this sort of defense will not satisfy the experimentalist, who will want to point out that, in any case, I cannot mean that *all* description is partial, since in order for me to have *noticed* this aspect of things, there must have been at least one exception. ("We don't know who discovered water, but it certainly wasn't a fish.") I confess that I do not quite understand this argument, for I cannot see how one can make rules that are more than introspective about the way in which we do not notice things. It seems to me that we do not give complete descriptions and definitions and I really cannot say how I came to notice it.

But to regard the statement that the processes of description and definition may be seen as partial (or that they may not be so seen) as either a definition or as an empirical statement is to mistake its *significance* in the argument. It is neither significantly a definition nor significantly an observation, but rather an admonition. And if the analytic-minded should still object, saying that if

nothing counts as complete in these areas, it adds nothing to say
that definition and description are partial, I protest that it
does—for *putting it this way* may promote certain values at the
expense of others.

* * *

The strategic viewpoint that I have outlined provides rhetorical
non-solutions to philosophical non-problems, i.e., solutions not so
much in the substance of the answers provided as in the approach
to the problems, and the spirit and structure of the answers. I will
illustrate two of them.

a. *The problem of universals.*

Socrates asked, "What is virtue?" And he would not accept
particular examples of virtuous acts as answers to his question.
Regardless of what you may think of the idealist's search, he was
in one sense right not to accept particular cases, for if we
reformulate his question as a linguistic one, it may be put: "How
can we name evidently different acts by the single name 'virtuous';
and how does a particular act qualify for the name?"—and you can
see that to enumerate cases is unresponsive to this question.
Socrates may be taken as looking for linguistic criteria or limits,
rather than ontological ones, and so to be asking, "What enables us
to name as we do?".

Please don't tell me that Socrates didn't intend his question this
way, unless you have a special metaphysical license and an
uninterpretable set of interpretations of his question, for otherwise, surely I may view it as a linguistic question. We may
distinguish this question from the *causal* question: "Why do we
name as we do?" Thus, the issue may be put rhetorically: "What
justifies us in naming as we do?" i.e., in grouping various
phenomena under one name and classifying particular phenomena
under one of many names.

Philosophical and psychological answers to this question range
from the radically operational (there need be no process of
justification at all), through the ordinary nominalistic (names are
purely arbitrary but culturally bounded); and the psychologistic
(perceived qualities determine names), to the purely idealistic (real
objects are alike or not, and so we name them so or not).

As you have no doubt guessed, the solution which I propose is a variant of psychologism—it is based upon analogy—but with a rhetorical twist—it is without perceptual limits. Outside of the context of argument, with another or with ourselves, I can find no serious objection to Humpty Dumpty's instant nominalism. But, in argument, I take it that to name is to make an analogy. One that is justified neither because the objects compared are *really* similar, nor because they must be *perceived* as similar, but only because you are persuaded that they *ought* to be taken as similar. Yet, if you ask what produces that persuasion, I can't tell you. Nor is that a particularly interesting rhetorical question, unless you think of rhetoric as a means to an end, and I shall direct you away from that view shortly.

This way of viewing the problem is different from radical operationism in that it requires justification; different from ordinary nominalism, in that it has no conventional limits; different from psychologism, in that it has no perceptual limits; and different from idealism, in that it has no ontological limits. The rhetorical perspective holds all limits and all naming arguable.

But is this an answer at all? In one way, yes; in another way, no. For it tells you where to look, but not what to look for. It suggests that you consult your *values* and your *imagination*.

b. *The problem of the analytic and the empirical.*

Various standards separate statements which are taken as purely analytic from those which are taken as empirical (or synthetic or factual), but the two usual ways of distinguishing the two sorts of statements are both concerned with logical considerations (truth and possibility). Thus, we normally distinguish statements which are true by virtue of the relations of their constituent parts, i.e., by virtue of meeting formal requirements, (e.g., "Seven is a number," where the notion of number is contained in the term "seven") from those the truth of which is determined by the facts of a situation, i.e., by meeting some physical condition (e.g., "My mother is in Chicago.").

Or, we distinguish *necessary* truths (which must be as they are, for any other state would be "impossible" in that it would render rational thought and discourse unapproachable) from *contingent* truths, that refer to some happenstance in the universe, which is as it is, but could be otherwise. The usual paradigms of analytic statements are the propositions of mathematics.

In an experimental age, there is another common distinction Analytic propositions are differentiated from empirical hypotheses on the basis that no tests would be appropriate to determine the truth of the former; i.e., tests would neither prove nor disprove them.

In all of these ways we want to say that the truth of some statements is determined by rules and that the truth of others is determined by facts.

There is a paradox at the heart of our way of regarding the realms of the analytic and the empirical. On the one hand, we want to say that the empirical (sense possibility) has really no limits; that anything *could* happen, and that our imposed and artificial definitions, which set limits, are *contained* within the sphere of empirical possibility. And yet it may also be cogently argued that the actual is some combination contained within the logically possible; i.e., that logical possibility contains empirical situations. These views are reflective of temperamental rather than logical differences as I hope to show you. For I believe that one can make a case both for the position that all statements are (importantly) analytic, and also for the position that all statements are (importantly) empirical. And, consequently, for the position that our means of verifying all statements should be *exclusively* one or the other.

The case for a purely analytic view may be briefly put thus: Since statements are made of words, and words are correctly or incorrectly used and related according to non-empirical criteria, the truth of all statements is analytic, at least in part, quite irrespective of empirical situations, and this dimension of judgment may be held to be primary, since no statement could be empirically *verifiable*, much less empirically *true*, without *first* meeting analytic tests. This argument is intended to dissociate meaning from experience, and is roughly comparable to the view that there can be nothing significantly contained in the answer to a question that is not contained in the question.

The case for an exclusively empirical view of language is less demanding, if less ingenious. The distinction between analytic and empirical statements fails if we regard analytic truths as empirical observations which have been much repeated (and this embraces even mathematical propositions if you regard them as confirmed by repetition through time). In this way, reason and experience are totally and finally conjoined with reason in the dependent role.

Or we may adopt any one of a number of negotiable positions. For instance, we might say that all statements fall somewhere on a continuum between the purely analytic and the purely empirical; or we may say that some statements are clearly one or the other and some fall into an indeterminate area. But if we choose to say that all statements possess both qualities in varying measures, we must still find a way to quantify how much of which quality each statement, or kind of statement, possesses, and how that quantity *operates* on the statement. And if we choose the view that there is a middle indeterminate ground, we still have the problem of boundaries—and now we even have more of them. We still lack a method of *handling* the problem.

What is it that will instruct us in characterizing less evident cases? Isn't it their similarity to empirical or analytical paradigms or established groups? And doesn't this reintroduce all of the elements of judgment and of analogy?

Consider the proposition that human beings are motivated by self-interest, or any post-Freudian psychological proposition. We could choose to evolve an analytic proof, based upon the notions of "being" and "self", or we could undertake extensive tests to determine how human beings behave. And, of course, either procedure may be challenged by the other. But on what grounds? What is the right way of doing it? It seems, in this case, that it is not the nature of the statement itself which determines its status, but our way of handling it. This means that analytic and empirical may be seen not as properties of statements, but rather as properties of investigators of statements.

Perhaps you think that it is just this sort of statement which permits this fluctuation; that this particular statement is in the indeterminate area and, therefore, variable. Let us apply the standards for analyticity to an apparently indisputable analytic proposition: that the same figure cannot be both square and circular.

Must this be an analytic proposition? *Can't* it be taken as an experiential proposition? What does it assert? It may assert that the definitions of square and circular are *mutually exclusive* (that the same figure cannot both have right angles and not have right angles); or that such figures cannot *exist* (which is to make of the definition on ontology); or that such figures cannot be *imagined*, which, absent an analogy between your mind and those of others, may be safely reduced to "*I* cannot imagine such figures." Or it may assert that nobody has ever seen such a figure, which, absent an analogy between your mind and those of others, may be safely reduced to "I have never seen such a figure".

The assertion that the same figure cannot both have right angles and not have them is based upon the laws of identity and non-contradiction, and shows that the speaker is willing to allow these metaphors to govern his experience. If it is asserted that such figures are unimaginable, I ask whether we know the boundaries of the imaginable—and do we know them *beforehand*? And if the proposition is taken to assert that the speaker has never seen such a figure, I ask whether he must have had all the experiences there are to have.

Suppose that I say that I have seen such a figure. Perhaps an operational test of the import of the assertion that this cannot be the case would be whether or not you ask me to inscribe it (but, n.b., to require that I inscribe it would be to require *another* step; it is now asked that it should be *communicated*). For if you ask me to inscribe it, you imply that if you saw it, you would believe that it did exist. But if you do not ask me to inscribe it, you are recording *your* determination to count *no* sense experience as evidence that it does exist (and your lack of curiosity; psychological curiosity if nothing else).

But surely, we want to say, there are some propositions to which testing is inappropriate. What does this assert? Let us put it variously: Tests of this proposition are unnecessary; tests of this proposition will not confirm or disprove it; tests of this proposition cannot establish or refute it, etc. What are these but ways of saying that the *speaker* feels no need of empirical verification or disverification? And isn't this only another way of saying that empirical evidence would not induce him to abandon or embrace the proposition?

But is that a universal law? Suppose that we laid a six foot man and a seven foot woman side by side and that the woman was perceptibly shorter than the man. I don't say that other hypotheses couldn't be tried (optical illusion, etc.) but having exhausted alternative explanations by other tests, what then? Isn't the telling question just whether you would abandon a precious proposition if some sense evidence contradicted it (and please don't tell me that the senses play tricks, for you would be ready enough to accept *confirmatory* sense evidence at least as comfort). Surely the question turns upon what you are *willing to accept* as evidence; which is to say, upon the investigator, and not the proposition.

If you say that a proposition remains analytic *until experience refutes it*, you really don't regard it as analytic at all. If you say that it must be so *regardless of experience*, aren't you only recording *your* determination not to allow any experience to refute it? The truth of any proposition may turn on rule or on experience as we will.

Thus, although we want to say that analytic statements hold come what may, I know of no statement which will hold come what may, unless we want it to, and any statement can be held come what may, if we make enough adjustments elsewhere. The truth of a statement need be determined neither by rules nor by facts. Statements are neither analytic nor empirical.

And this, of course, includes the statement that statements are neither analytic nor empirical, for, of course, I am engaged in persuasion as much as if I had set exclusive limits. And, as before, the issue is neither epistemological nor ontological, but axiological, i.e., a question of what sorts of values one wishes to promote in the inescapable hierarchy.

4. *Rhetoric may be reformulated as an end in itself.*

At last, as I promised, arguments and justification dissolve and we are left alone in an empty room with only our attitudes and our values for support. And I am tempted to end here and leave you to draw your own conclusions, but that would do too much violence to my didactic tendencies and (perhaps) to your expectations. I have been promising throughout to tell you where the tunnel ends.

A popular dramatic explication-for-all-occasions is that every tragedy is in some sense a failure of communication among characters. The tragedy of rhetoric may be not that we *fail* to communicate, but rather that we *expect* to communicate.

* * *

Aristotle defines rhetoric as the faculty of finding, in a particular case, the available means of persuasion. But he can't mean *all* of the available means because *beforehand*, everything and anything might count as a potential means of persuasion. Therefore, we must select from among the available means. But how to select? We want to say that we do it pragmatically, with a particular end in mind, and that the end is always persuasion of others—which implies communication. But I hope to have shown you that we don't know what, if anything, brings about communication either before or after the alleged fact. Tests have been deified by modern behaviorist theories of rhetoric and persuasion, and perhaps that is appropriate to a procedure with metaphysical foundations.

Thus, the element common to some ancient and to all modern rhetorical theories is the emphasis upon the other (with the exception possibly of Kenneth Burke's notion of identification) and the consequent, tacitly assumed, primary value of inter-subjectivity, so that it seems to us now that rhetoric, as a process, and persuasion and communication, as results, must necessarily be conjoined for the former to have point. But why ought rhetoric to imply communication? And why ought it to imply two or more persons *necessarily*? I am not suggesting solipsism or anything like it, and I will meet the charge shortly.

Communication is not the only *possible* goal of language-using and perhaps it is not even the most *important* one. Tallyrand said that providence gave men the gift of speech so that they might conceal their thoughts. But that is not at all what I mean; nor am I recommending that view (except, perhaps, in some cases, in its more subtle meaning of concealing one's thoughts of the tre-mendum from oneself) for that is only to say that different messages are being sent. They are still primarily messages sent to others, and so communication of something to others is still primary. This only shifts the purpose from one variation on the theme of attaining power over others to another variation. I mean, rather, that language may be used as a way of attaining stasis—or its contrary, excitation—for oneself.

What I am suggesting is that language may be seen to be rather more like a mace than like a rapier—as having many points and edges which need penetrate little to accomplish their purpose, rather than as having a single point which we demand should penetrate deeply. I am suggesting that rhetoric need not *neces-sarily* be conjoined with communication.

The argument that language-using must be inextricably inter-woven with communication usually rests on some variant of the social-tool approach to language, normally beginning with the assertion that we learned our language in a community. I cannot see how we might know how we learned our language—though I can understand the documentation of attempts at teaching it—without intuiting ourselves languageless or asking the language-less in order to find out. But in any case, assent to the proposition that language is *acquired* communally is not assent to the proposition that it must be *used* communally. Remember that it is in the interests of "communication" to efface variations among individuals—and that may be too high a price to pay.

* * *

Aristotle's *Rhetoric* begins, "Rhetoric is the counterpart of dialectic." "Counterpart", here, is usually taken to mean something that serves to complement or *complete* the other thing, but it may also mean a part or thing *corresponding* to another. Since we do not know what, if anything, causes persuasion, rhetoric might be dialectic, and I am about to argue that, in one sense, it ought to be.

I propose to define (or redefine, if you will) rhetoric as the art of manipulating analogies, where analogy and dysanalogy are seen as merger and division. And to define persuasion as the art of urging one perspective rather than another. These definitions have at least two important consequences. They rob rhetoric and persuasion of their objectivity and they divorce rhetoric and persuasion from necessary conjunction with communication. But you may say that they also rob rhetoric and persuasion of significance and divorce them from any reason to be used. I hope to show you that this need not be so.

Why practice rhetoric *consciously* (since in my view, we can't use language without doing so) if we can't know its effects? There are several ways to answer. You may be saying, "If he really thinks that communication through language is an illusion, why does he talk to me?" But it is no good saying to the solipsist, "If you think I don't exist, why do you tell me so?" Any number of existential answers will do. He could answer that it is his nature, that it seemed a good idea at the time, or that he must do something. But in any case, there is no solipsism here, for although solipsism is not ruled out, (i.e., my sensations may be internally caused, or not caused at all) I am nowhere suggesting that we doubt the evidence of our senses, only particular *interpretations* of that evidence. We need not doubt the existence of others, merely that we ought to say with certitude and finality that we know what another is. Above all, I doubt that one must accept, unquestioningly, the rules of others in making those interpretations.

Thus, it is neither an ontological nor an epistemological problem at base, but an axiological one. And the desired effect of the sort of attitude that I am suggesting is not necessarily to change the *direction* of rhetoric but to change our standpoint from an exclusively other-centered one, and thus to change the *standard* by which rhetoric is evaluated.

To the psychologically sophisticated, paranoid-schizophrenia suggests itself. The uses of paranoia are many and, to the extent that the social contract is now so thoroughly binding, a little corrective may not be altogether out of place. But I will not endorse schizophrenia. For, although a schizophrenic is largely impervious to criticism because he does not invent any outside authority to justify his way of experiencing (and this is a strength inasmuch as it makes him self-reliant and psychologically self-sustaining) his weakness is obvious. He cannot ask a question to which he doesn't already know the answer and he is a monument to intolerance. He has merely replaced the tyranny of an *externally* imposed system (convention) with the tyranny of an *internally* imposed inflexibility.

* * *

Nor is this position even skeptical, in a strong or complete sense, for I am not suggesting that all efforts to know whether we communicate are futile; nor that we don't communicate; nor that we couldn't find out. (I hope that I haven't had all of the experiences there are to have.) Although in particular cases, I am indeed skeptical. People are always telling me with great authority that they know things that I don't see how they can know. It is the attitude of authority which gives me pause. Ask yourself whether you would despise those who hold even the most despicable positions in your judgment if their attitude and tone were of uncertainty and question. If you will do yourself the great favor of pretending that you don't know anything, I think you may soon discover that, in many cases, you are not pretending.

* * *

Throughout these inquiries, I have been telling you on what grounds I think you ought not to be persuaded, and now I can clearly specify those upon which I think you *should* be finally and certainly persuaded. None at all. It is just the certitude and finality of science and convention to which this rhetorical view is antidote. So basic is this attitude to rhetoric that there should be a sign

94

above the rhetorician's door—abandon truth all ye who enter here.

It is this variety of agnosticism which I am urging, and it is difficult to tire of agnosticism. (Indeed it is the only perspective, I think, of which one cannot tire, because one can foray out of agnosticism and one may enjoy the foray *qua* foray, whereas, from any other perspective, it would be a departure, and so, a diminution.)

I can only hope that the social by-product of this pervasive tentativeness would not be palsy but tolerance, for tolerance ought to be uncertainty's companion. (I remind you that wars are seldom directed by those having tentative views.) And, of course, flatulence may be avoided by active consideration of any perspective (please notice the absence of the qualifier "reason-able") for tolerance, should it be promoted by this view, need by no means be the biggest return on the investment.

Philosophy begins in wonder; at least it used to. But rhetoric is wonder itself. Consider yourself alongside the modern computer. It is more powerful, usually larger, in many cases more beautiful and more sought after than you. The one thing that you can do that the computer cannot is to question yourself in certain ways. And that is not because the computer which would speculate cannot be built, but because there would be no point in building it. The computer is the ultimate anti-tolerance instrument. It gives *the* answer, or a *definite* range of answers, and cannot function with ambiguity or paradox. In short, it is built to achieve decision; and if it is a danger to humanity, it is not because it is *more* efficient than men, but because it is efficient *at all*; because it enshrines the decision process itself.

Language-using is so often analogized to the computer's function that I cannot resist the view that the analogy is suspect. That is my usual response to usual metaphors. Could it be that we conceive language incorrectly, or at least incompletely; that language may function to *avoid* final decision—not to *relate* information, but to *create* it. This is not an apology for revelry in speculation alone, but rather for speculation as instrument, not of decision, but of discovery and not a discovery of answers, but of new questions. The world of your mind might not be a bounded and finite memory bank, nor its function completely programmed.

* * *

For everything you get, you must pay with something else. I think that many have surrendered the uses of imagination for effect upon others. If this is so, the price is too high and the prize may be illusory.

I see convention and the modern emphasis on objectivism and decision as a huge machine that consumes individual imagination. The nature of convention prohibits us from modifying it, and so we must either allow it to go on undisturbed, or destroy it. The former alternative rests upon the argument that order (which usually means what I am comfortable with) is the prime good, and confusion (which usually means that with which I am uncomfortable) is the paramount evil.

If disease and accident are the great killers of the life of the body, ease and habit are the great killers of the life of the mind. Endless curiosity is valuable even where answers seem unattainable. After all, it is only habit which conjoins question and answer.

Concrete meaning is what sometimes seems missing when attention and question are focused. And what causes the frustration connected with this loss can only be our vanity—the idea that anything can resist our attention is maddening. It may be that language, or life itself, has meaning only if that meaning is not sought. Even if this is so, the search is more important than the meaning.

Curiosity may have killed the cat, but at least the cat had lived.

Toward a Rhetorical Theory of Language: Parallels Between the Work of John Macksoud and Jacques Derrida

In the fall of 1964, at the invitation of the Chancellor of the University of California at Santa Barbara (UCSB), Kenneth Burke became that year's Regent Lecturer and delivered four speeches at Campbell Hall. These lectures, which were read by Burke from prepared texts, became chapters two through five of *Language as Symbolic Action*—subsequently published in 1966. In 1964, John Macksoud had become the newest member of the faculty in the UCSB Speech Department. He had just been awarded his doctorate in speech communication from the University of California at Los Angeles and had completed work on a dissertation entitled *The Literary Theories of Kenneth Burke and the Discovery of Meanings in Oral Interpretation*. Before arriving at UCSB in the fall of 1964, Burke had acquired and read a copy of Macksoud's dissertation. During the course of Burke's lectureship, the two men met and began a long friendship. In their first meeting, making reference to Macksoud's dissertation, Burke is reputed to have said to Macksoud: "You are the only one who has understood me." This remarkable compliment from Burke serves as a persuasive recommendation for Macksoud's work and raises the inevitable question: why is Macksoud's writing not more prominent in the fields associated with language and communication theory? The primary answer lies in the fact that Macksoud's academic career was relatively brief, and during that period, his publications in language theory, although provocative and of high quality, were not numerous.

Failing to get tenure in the Speech Department at UCSB, Macksoud accepted a position in the English department at the State University of New York at Binghamton in 1973. The central reason given for the denial of reappointment and promotion to associate professor was "two negative reviews of an unpublished manuscript by anonymous readers solicited by the administration" (*UCSB Daily Nexus*, May 23, 1972). The unfair practice of anonymous reviewing led to a lawsuit against the University, which, as Craig Smith reports in his Introduction, was decided in favor of Macksoud and granted him a one year extension of his contract. However, rather than continue the dispute with the University, Macksoud decided to accept the position at the State University of New York. The "unpublished manuscript" in question was *Other Illusions: Inquiries Toward a Rhetorical Theory*, self-published by Macksoud in 1973. It prompted considerable controversy at the time it was written, continues to be controversial, and is, of course, the occasion for this book.

After his departure to New York, a letter to Macksoud written by former students presented a reason to cite Burke's memorable line where he says, "The universe would appear to be something like a cheese. It can be sliced an infinite number of ways" (1984, 136). Keeping with the scale of this thought, a postscript was added asking, facetiously, whether Macksoud believed the universe was plastic or elastic. In a reply a few days later, he concluded with a postscript that contained a two word answer to the students' question: "probably yes." Even though the exchange was initiated in jest, this answer seemed, at the time, as responsive as no response. But, over time, this response has appreciated in value.

One of the more telling tests of philosophical inclinations lies in the nature of replies to either/or questions. It was said of the Buddha that he would not allow himself to be trapped by bivalent logic. Resisting the seduction of this logic gave rise to the questioning and answering found in Zen Buddhist koans. Macksoud's koan-like answer suggests compatibility with eastern spiritual attitudes. The traditions of mysticism of both East and West offer examples of alternatives or supplements to the either/or logic generally attributed to the Western tradition beginning with the Greeks. The contrast between these two logics centers on the way in which oppositional relation is understood. Macksoud explores precisely this oppositional logic and how it concerns issues of identification, relationship, and relativity. He does so, not by drawing externally on Eastern or mystical traditions, but by pushing internally on the Western rational tradition. He turns reason on itself to expose a black hole in the ether of rationality, opening passage to another logic. In this regard, Macksoud independently matches all the major moves and countermoves made by Jacques Derrida in the evolution of deconstruction as a postmodern assessment of language. The similarity in their views is remarkable, especially when considering they were doing their groundbreaking work independently of each other at approximately the same time from the mid-1960s to the early 1970s.

Since the essentials of what Macksoud borrows from Kenneth Burke's reflections on language—particularly the early Burke's pluralist emphasis on the pervasiveness of perspective, metaphor, and analogy—are thoroughly presented in Macksoud's dissertation, the following will focus on comparison of Macksoud and Derrida in three central areas of overlap in their respective investigations of language: the literal and the metaphoric, the laws of language, and the question of relativity. This comparison shows how certain features of deconstructive thinking have an indigenous point of origin in the work of an American rhetorical theorist and why this thinking remains a necessary and seminal part not only of the future of rhetorical theory, but of all the disciplines in the humanities and sciences as these rely on language and symbolism.

The Literal and the Metaphoric

The distinction between the literal and the metaphoric serves as a decisive intersection for the transition to an alternative logic of oppositional relation as well as for the similarity between Macksoud and Derrida. An examination of arguments Macksoud employs in work published after his dissertation serves to more clearly draw out the points of comparison to Derrida's deconstructive approach. Upholding a rigid distinction between the literal or explicit meaning of a text and the metaphorical or more implicit meanings of texts requires being able, at the very least, to provide some hard examples of literal meaning. In this regard, consider Macksoud's "Mr. Jones is watching television" example taken from an essay published in *Philosophy and Rhetoric* in 1971:

> It is obvious that there is difficulty in determining implicit or unsaid meanings, but can the explicit meaning of a…text be construed to the satisfaction of most intelligent minds? I invite you to consider this sentence. "Mr. Jones is watching television." It seems at first that we have no difficulty in construing the explicit meaning of this sentence, but consider these problems. The word "Mr." implies that the person doing the watching is male. Are there criteria for maleness which are fixed? If so, can you give an explicit list of those criteria, and will your list always be a mere *repetition* of what it was yesterday, and will it be a *reiteration* of mine…? [emphasis added]. "Mr. Jones" normally implies membership in the race of man, which entails another set of explicit criteria. Yet another set of criteria is involved with the specific identity of Mr. Jones. Do we mean Mr. Jones' body is watching television (And if so, without which bodily parts, in which arrangement, would he cease to be Mr. Jones?), or are certain aspects of personality involved, and if so, which? Consider the phrase "is watching." What are the explicit criteria for the act of watching? Suppose, for instance, that Mr. Jones looks away for one-half second each hour, or each minute, or each second. Is he then not watching television, and when does he again begin? Does watching involve mental acts which are no part of the overt behavior of Mr. Jones, as

for example, thinking, concentrating, attending? Surely an objective explication of this sentence would involve generating all of these criteria and many
more. (Macksoud, 1971, 142-143)

A quick reply to this example might assert that, by a bizarre method of dis-
section, Macksoud has rendered problematic a straightforward English sentence
that accomplishes a simple communication. But the issue is: does this sentence
reliably convey one literal meaning? On close scrutiny, its monolithic simplicity
dissolves into an endless stream of fragments. When pressed, this example of
explicit meaning appears to be yet another example of implicit meaning and, as
such, does no more than suggest meanings through analogical extension. Full and
hard criteria for singular meanings, the identities of the terms, are not available.

According to Macksoud, the possibility of "objective explication" or "objective meaning" operates as a crucial assumption in most theories of communication. For the communication of an objective meaning to occur, something very
much like a stimulus-response or causal connection must exist between words and
their meanings or identities. Demonstrating such a relationship requires showing
that, through various repetitions, the same words or combination of words trigger
the same response. The words (the stimuli) must carry with them a set of instructions (criteria) sufficient to insure they will be consistently and properly applied
(the response). Macksoud argues that even where a particular use of words appears to produce a desired response, the *operative* stimulus may not be solely
or self-evidently the words uttered. Where communication is the issue in question, the link between words and meanings cannot be assumed. Similar responses
may only appear to be similar and may have been generated by the *same* words
concealing *different* operative stimuli in the form of *different sets of instructions*
being triggered by those words. The question may then arise as to *which* set of
instructions or criteria were actually attended to and followed? When submitted
to Macksoud's kind of analysis, it becomes easier to see that the sentence "Mr.
Jones is watching television" may convey a range and a variety of meanings as a
result of having no explicit meaning—that is, no one set of instructions necessarily attached to the words.

Macksoud would alter the flow chart for communication contained in the
model described above to include the ever-present possibilities for miscommuni-
cation. As an alternative to this chart, he might propose the following description:
The words (the apparent stimuli) carry with them *more than one* set of instructions (only one set of which becomes the operative stimulus in a particular case)
for how they will be applied, thereby producing the circumstance that no particular application (the response, the meaning) can be guaranteed. These possibilities
reveal how the application of words merges with the issue of identity. If words

are like instructions and the instructions do not carry out themselves, then the identity of words is split and divided by the multiple paths by which they may be "followed" or applied. Identity is split by difference.

In *Other Illusions*, Macksoud explains why neither scientific method nor any other conceivable method can hope to demonstrate causal connections between words and meanings by isolating the operative stimulus. Such isolation is precluded by the problem of repetition—one of the problems identified (with emphasis added) in the "Mr. Jones is watching television" example. Macksoud observes that "only by repetition do we generate explanation," or, in this case, meaning. But in the same breath he notes that "we cannot repeat the past" (1973, 14). Here he identifies an omnipresent paradox of life especially relevant to language: only by repetition can meaning be generated or reproduced, but the nature of the unfolding of time is such that repetition is not possible. Repetition of the same, as the identical, is an illusion.

Both sameness *and* difference are irreducible components of repetition. Those who investigate any phenomenon have only comparison and contrast, not identity, as fundamental tools. With amazing, and some might argue perverse, dexterity of argument Macksoud illustrates how scientific method, as with any mode of description, is founded on analogy and dysanalogy—on human, often all too human, judgments of likeness and non-likeness:

> Perform and repeat this experiment. Ask a willing and capable subject to make a fist and observe his response. Let us suppose that he performs an operation which satisfies the command...Suppose that you allege that the verbal command stimulated the response, but I argue that it was the presence of a shadow falling across the subject's face. Repeating the test—and I do not mean to say that we could do so without altering *anything*—would be useless. I suppose that you will want to remove the shadow and produce the response again. Suppose that you do. On this test, I hypothesize that it was the pinch of a tight left shoe that caused the response. Very well, you will remove the left shoe, and reproduce the response. But on this test, I hypothesize that it was a cramped position of the coccyx that produced the response. Let me suppose that you will run out of patience before I run out of hypotheses. What are we to do? On what ground are we to prefer the verbal stimulus to the other hypothesized stimuli? It is clear that we must now state grounds upon which hypotheses should be accepted. But, n. b., if we do, we reduce the question to one of persuasiveness. (1973, 14-15)

Macksoud goes on to address standard complaints that might be raised regarding this line of argument, parrying counter-arguments invoking past experience, methods of concomitant variation, and other objections. With his arguments

Macksoud desires to emphasize the various problems rooted in the assumptions underlying the use of repetition in scientific method. These assumptions include the following: the tacit assumption that all the possible operative stimuli can be tested and controlled, the assumption that the relevant stimuli can be identified (noting that the criteria for relevance are derived by way of the method in question), and the assumption that a single variable, conspicuously present in a group of tests, ought to be preferred as an explanation over several different variables. Assumptions are not absent in any line of inquiry, but these particular assumptions permit Macksoud to conclude that even scientific method is a form of argument by analogy rather than a form of conclusive and demonstrative proof. Since testing, like the use of language, requires repetition and since with each repetition something new is present, the strict control of variables is inherently impossible.

That the same words may refer in different directions appears to constitute an inescapable and, thereby, essential feature of language. But will not careful attention to context reveal that the words point in one direction in particular uses? The wealth of information present in context may provide a way of fixing the current use of words. It would seem that Macksoud's "Mr. Jones is watching television" example would not be very problematic if more of the context in which the statement was made were available. But how exactly does context help? Consider another of Macksoud's examples, this one taken from his discussion of the process of interpreting a verbal act:

> We want to say that we infer the motives and significance of an act from its *context* in roughly the way in which we say that we infer the meaning of a word from its context. Imagine that on a warm day a normally attired man of ordinary appearance knocks on your door, and when you open it, he says, "I love birdseed." How shall we go about interpreting this behavior? If you object that it is impossible to pass judgment on an act pulled out of context in this way, I ask you to remember that nothing can be *out of context*--only *in another context*...But you want to know more about the context. Suppose I add that it is Saturday, July, and high noon...does that help? If I continue to add observations of this sort will you have *more* context, a more *complete* context—or only a *different* one? Would it help you to know that he had blue eyes? I can continue to make such observations indefinitely, but surely it is not necessary that you have all aspects of the context given before you can construct a hypothesis to explain his behavior. Indeed, you *could not* have more than a selection of data. Of course what you want to know is the relevant details of the context. But doesn't that assume that there is either a *standard* criterion for relevance or some *particular* way of determining relevance in this case? Relevance is a *transitive* relationship. (1973, 32)

The context attended to is always less than the available context and the process of selection occurs on the basis of a judgment about what may be relevant to the interpretation of an element within the context. And this judgment is not informed by an intransitive set of rules. If nothing can be out of context, and context is in some sense always a selection or division of itself, then there is no *context* but only *contexts*. As Macksoud explains, every issue of context resembles the problem of the limits of a text:

> The problem of the scope of the contextual frame is analogous to the problem of textual construction faced by literary analysts. You will find persons who advocate interpreting the meaning of a word in a poem in the context of the line in which it appears; in the context of the sentence or stanza; in the context of the whole poem; in the context of other works by the same author; in the context of the literary output of its period; in the context of its geographic or ethnic origins; and in the context of all literary and human experience. (1973, 34)

Identifying the meaning of a word or sentence is hooked into the problem of identifying the context in which it appears. Context does not have a self-evident boundary. Since each word relates outwardly to words and referents other than itself, and since these relations extend into contexts of shifting and malleable boundaries, how could the repetition of words *not* be essentially involved in something more than a repetition of the same? And how could this sameness be anything other than analogy, that is, connection by way of the similar but not the identical and self-same?

For Macksoud, the field of language is a continuum not divided by essentially different kinds of events as is postulated in the traditional distinction between literal and metaphoric uses of language:

> I suspect that, in use, the word "literally" is only a way of adding emphasis and, if it is not, it ought to be, for where it is used to enshrine certain perspectives, I ask whether we have a uniform way to grade similarities and differences. Looking at language-using in this way allows us to say that any use of a word may be seen as equally literal or metaphoric with any other use, and to abandon the dualistic perspective of two *kinds* of language, one discursive (scientific) and one presentational (poetic), with which we are usually encumbered, and by which vast areas of intellectual activity are assigned to art, as contrasted (usually invidiously) with science. (1973, 72-73)

The tenor and the sequence of Macksoud's arguments about language may be traced similarly in Derrida's work, especially in his 1977 exchange with John Searle in the pages of *Glyph*. Discussing intention and its role as a criterion in identifying serious and literal speech, Derrida finds that the material sign cannot fully convey and present intention in the sense of guaranteeing that intention:

> I am…in agreement with…[Searle's] statement, "…there is no getting away from intentionality, because *a meaningful sentence is just a standing possibility of the corresponding (intentional) speech act*" (p. 202). I would, on the other hand, add, placing undue and artificial emphasis on *ful* [in the word "meaning*ful*"] that for reasons just stated, there cannot be a "sentence" that is fully and actually meaningful and hence (or because) there can be no "corresponding (intentional) speech act" that would be fulfilled, fully present, active and actual. Thus, the value of the act (used so generally and analyzed so little in the theory of speech acts), like that of event, should be submitted to systematic questioning. As in the entire philosophical tradition that supports it, this value implies that of presence which I have proposed to defer to questions of differential…iterability. (1977, 195-196)

Derrida goes on to explain the role of iterability, which parallels Macksoud's discussion of how the identity of a word is split through repeated applications (iterations):

> The intention of the speaker, one might think, is closest to, if not absolutely present in what is said. Yet nothing is less certain…(p. 201). Once again, iterability makes possible idealization—and thus, a certain identity in repetition that is independent of the multiplicity of factual events—while at the same time limiting the idealization it makes possible: broaching and breaching it at once…To put it more simply and more concretely: at the very moment… when someone would like to say or to write, "On the twentieth of September 1793 I set out on a journey from London to Oxford," the very factor that will permit the mark (be it psychic, oral, graphic) to function beyond this moment—namely the possibility of its being repeated another time—breaches, divides, expropriates the "ideal" plenitude or self-presence of intention, of meaning (to say) and, *a fortiori*, of all adequation between meaning and saying. Iterability alters, contaminating parasitically what it identifies and enables to repeat "itself." (1977, 200)

Similar to Macksoud, Derrida then proceeds to show the effect this phenomenon of iterability has on the way in which opposition is understood:

> The iterability of the mark does not leave any of the philosophical oppositions which govern the idealizing abstraction intact (for instance, serious/non-serious, literal/metaphorical or sarcastic, ordinary/parasitical, strict/non-strict, etc.). Iterability blurs *a priori* the dividing line that passes between these opposed terms, "corrupting" it if you like, contaminating it parasitically, qua limit. What is re-markable about the mark includes the margin within the mark. The line delineating the margin can therefore never be de-

termined rigorously, it is never pure and simple. The mark is re-markable in that it "is" also its margin...Even if it only threatens with a perpetually possible parasitism, this menace is inscribed *a priori* in the limit. It divides the dividing-line and its unity at once. (1977, 209-210)

That the mark also contains within it its margin, its other, is, ironically, a paradoxical situation that exposes the limitations of words with respect to the task of description. However, within this discussion, Derrida brings into focus the intimate connection between iterability and context, which parallels the similar movement in Macksoud's thinking. Here Derrida is quoting himself from his essay "Signature, Event, Context":

"As far as the internal semiotic context is concerned, the force of the rupture is no less important: by virtue of its essential iterability, a written syntagma can always be detached from the chain in which it is inserted or given without causing it to lose all possibility of functioning...One can perhaps come to recognize other possibilities in it by inscribing it or *grafting* it onto other chains. No context can entirely enclose it. Nor any code, the code here being both the possibility and impossibility of writing, of its essential iterability (repetition/alterity)" (p. 182). And: "...in so doing [i.e. by the iterability or the citationality that it permits] it [the sign] can break with every given context, engendering an infinity of new contexts in a manner which is absolutely illimitable. This does not imply that the mark is valid outside of a context, but on the contrary that there are only contexts without any center or absolute anchoring [*ancrage*]" (pp. 185-6). (1977, 203-204)

This, of course, echoes Macksoud's statement quoted above that "nothing can be *out of context—only in another context.*"

Macksoud's arguments and examples illustrate the problem of boundaries. How may precise distinctions between this and that get drawn? Macksoud has shown that discrete divisions between the literal and non-literal and between text and context are more than merely difficult to draw; they are, by best estimates, simply unavailable in practice. Derrida shares the same conclusion: "I try to show not only that the ideal purity of the distinctions proposed (by Searle, for example) is inaccessible, but also that its practice would necessitate excluding certain essential traits of what it claims to explain and describe" (1988, 117).

This line of argument would appear to slide irretrievably toward the precipice looming in the objection that where there are no rigorous distinctions there are no distinctions at all. And, surprising many, while explaining himself in the "Afterword" to *Limited Inc*, Derrida makes the following admission:

I confirm it: for me, from the point of view of theory and of the concept, "unless a distinction can be made rigorous and precise it isn't really a distinction." (1988, 126)

This admission would appear to be contradicted by Derrida on, for example, the following occasion as well as numerous other occasions:

Iterability *blurs a priori* the dividing line that passes between these opposed terms…"corrupting" it if you like, contaminating it parasitically, qua limit… The line delineating the margin can therefore *never be determined rigorously*, it is never pure and simple [emphasis added]. (1977, 210; see, for example, also 217, 223, 226, and 246)

In light of what Derrida says in the previous citation, this admission suggests that he may have painted himself into the corner of asserting, in apparent contradiction, that indeed distinctions between words cannot be made "rigorous and precise," and therefore, these distinctions are not really distinctions.

What can "never be determined rigorously" might also be thought to be synonymous with the phrase "always indeterminate." But Derrida has also spoken in what appears to be a contradictory way on this point as well: "I do not believe I have ever spoken of 'indeterminacy,' whether in regard to 'meaning' or anything else" (1988, 148). More than likely these difficulties arise for Derrida partly by way of the process of translation, but it is not especially helpful for him to deny applicability of any and every notion of indeterminacy with respect to the boundary of meaning in light of the way in which he has described the effects of iterability. But it is important, nevertheless, not to miss the point he is making in the midst of such apparent contradictions. This point becomes clear in what Derrida says immediately following the remark about having never spoken of indeterminacy, and his clarification does much to resolve the confusion:

Undecidability is something else again. While referring to what I have said above and elsewhere, I want to recall that undecidability is always a *determinate* oscillation between possibilities (for example, of meaning, but also of acts). These possibilities are themselves highly *determined* in strictly *defined* situations (for example, discursive—syntactical or rhetorical—but also political, ethical, etc.). They are *pragmatically* determined…I say "undecidability" rather than "indeterminacy" because I am interested more in relations of force, in differences of force, in everything that allows, precisely, determinations in given situations to be stabilized through a decision of writing…There would be no indecision or *double bind* were it not between *determined* (semantic, ethical, political) poles, which are upon occasion terribly necessary and always irreplaceably singular. Which is to say that from the point of view of semantics, but also of ethics and politics, "deconstruction" should never lead either to relativism or to any sort of indeterminism. (1988, 148)

What has been revealed to be an apparent *indeterminacy* Derrida wants to redefine as an oscillating *undecidability* between highly determined possibilities "in strictly defined situations." As will be discussed in more detail below, these oscillations involve a shifting of context, which creates alternative meanings and readings. And Derrida is right to point out that this *multiplication* of (determinate) meaning is importantly different from indeterminate meaning or approximate meaning. This point emerges again in his discussion of the concept.

> Every concept that lays claim to any rigor whatsoever implies the alternative of "all or nothing"...Even the concept of "difference of degree," the concept of relativity is, qua concept, determined according to the logic of all or nothing, of yes or no: differences of degree or nondifference of degree. It is impossible or illegitimate to form a *philosophical concept* outside this logic of all or nothing...To this oppositional logic...without which the distinction and the limits of a concept have no chance, I oppose nothing, least of all a logic of approximation...a simple empiricism of difference in degree; rather I add a supplementary complication that calls for other concepts, for other thoughts beyond the concept and another form of "general theory," or rather another discourse, another "logic" that accounts for the impossibility of concluding such a "general theory." This other discourse doubtless takes into account the conditions of this classical and binary logic, but it no longer depends entirely upon it. (1988, 116-117)

Bivalent either/or logic cannot be entirely abandoned any more than traditional metaphysics can be completely discredited, but it can be supplemented by an additional logic—a logic that takes into consideration the troubling, the oscillation, of meaning through the effects of iterability and recontextualization. Derrida's arguments, like Macksoud's, signal a breakdown or rupture in the universality of Aristotelian notions of non-contradiction and causality. The meanings of words are *overdetermined*, making possible oscillations whereby identities of terms are more than singularly discrete and relations between them are more than causal.

With their assault on the boundary between the opposition of the literal and the metaphoric, Derrida and Macksoud arrive at the possibility of saying that nothing precludes seeing all uses of language as the same in kind. At the level of theory all uses may be seen as equally literal or equally metaphoric. All uses are fraught with the same mix of difficulties and advantages arising through repetition—repetition with a difference.

The use of the word "all" signals a uniformity of effect characteristic of a law. Such a notion of all-inclusive uniformity contrasts with the Aristotelian view of law, which includes not only that which occurs without exception, but also that which happens with regularity or "as a rule." The first great departure from this Aristotelian fabric of laws/rules to the understanding of phenomena by way of exceptionless laws occurs with Newton and the laws of motion derived from the work of Galileo and Kepler. What Galileo discovered about motion received thorough formulation by Newton. In Aristotle's cosmology an essential difference exists between "heavenly bodies" and "earthly bodies," but Newton exposes the sense in which all bodies are of the same kind and all motion of the same type. The difficulty resides not in seeing a difference between the cyclical motion of the moon moving around the earth and the linear motion of an apple falling from a tree, but rather in seeing a way in which these essentially different motions are also the same. For Newton, varieties of motion all become differences of the same: sameness differed.

Newton's new understanding of motion provided a model for every opposition, polarity, and dialectic; the contrast can be seen not as an agon between two discrete and separate entities or qualities, but as a relation or continuum between two extremes. Here it is important to fully appreciate the word "continuum" in its paradoxical sense. The *Oxford English Dictionary* defines "continuum" as "a set or series of elements passing into each other, the parts of which cannot be distinguished clearly except by arbitrary division." The word "elements" alludes to that which is discrete or elemental but which, nevertheless, cannot be clearly separated from other elements. Expressed in another way, the continuum is both one differing itself in multiple ways and two always participating one in the other—paradoxically both two and one, both the many and the one. The classical notion of discrete division models an oppositional relation whereby the two sides are marked by *essential difference*. In the continuum model, the two sides are also marked by *essential relation*—a relation whereby one cannot be what it is without the other and neither can be reduced to the other.

This notion of lawfulness advanced by Newton requires the shift from the view of opposites as discrete essences (such as "heavenly" and "earthly" bodies; circular and linear motion) to the view of opposites as paradoxical interpenetrations of two sides which are both *essentially different* (one may not be reduced to the other) and *essentially related* (one does not occur without the other) as, for example, in Newton's cosmology—centripetal and centrifugal forces and gravity and inertia. The scientific revolution spawned by Newton is evidence of the power of this orientation (for an extensive treatment of this subject, see Desilet, 1999). In the case of the difference between the literal and the metaphoric, Derrida and

Macksoud converge on an alternative insight into oppositional relation marking the qualitative shift that may be seen as merely an extension of Enlightenment thinking. Both then apply this view of oppositional relation with a thoroughness that results in the postmodern difference.

Laws of Language

In the postmodern way of thinking, opposites may now be understood to belong to a kind of uniformity or continuum that is not a feature of the Aristotelian paradigm. Following the arguments of Derrida and Macksoud, the departure from the Aristotelian logic of opposites prepares the way for the formulation of an all-inclusive law of language. In the attempt to understand the workings of language, it is especially important to keep in mind the paradoxical nature of the relation between opposites proposed by Macksoud and Derrida. As Derrida expresses it, "Iterability blurs a priori the dividing line that passes between… opposed terms." This "blurring" must be carefully understood in the sense of a continuum whereby opposites are *neither* discrete *nor* merged, or they are *both* discrete *and* merged. In the form of an inclusive principle operative in discourse, it may be stated as follows:

> The First Law of Language (The Law of Signification): As the process whereby linguistic meaning arises, signification is necessarily a consequence of the disposition of words in contingent contextual configuration as that includes the broader linguistic and nonlinguistic environment. An immediate corollary to this law follows: Signification is uniform in kind among all uses of language.

This First Law of Language resembles Newton's First Law of Motion in two respects: 1) it overcomes a strict dualism of types of meaning (for example, the literal and the metaphoric), and 2) it places every word under the influence of a *context* of words, acts, events, and physical environment. Recall that Newton's First Law, the Law of Inertia, states that "Every body continues in its state of rest, or uniform motion in a straight line, unless it is compelled to change that state by force impressed upon it" (as paraphrased in Heidegger, 1977, 256). The expression "every body" indicates that motion is not derived differently for different bodies. The phrase "by force impressed upon it" indicates the influence of *context*, of the field of other bodies, on the motion of a given body.

Put in Newtonian terms, the First Law of Language could be explained in the following way: The meaning or intent of a word, left to itself, remains dormant or constant unless altered by the influence of other words. But since words always reside in the shifting context of other words, meaning remains exposed and susceptible to alteration. The relation between intention and context is analogous to that between inertia and gravity; meaning, like motion, is an intersection of influences. The literal meaning of a word could be understood, like the body left to itself moving uniformly in a straight line, as a kind of intention independent of context. But being out of context in this sense, as Macksoud and Derrida have argued, is not possible—just as it is not possible for a physical body to be out of the context of all other bodies in Newtonian physics.

However, it should be quickly added that neither Derrida nor Macksoud is an uncritical advocate of Enlightenment science. In fact, Macksoud taught, as part of his lectures on the "Limits of Language," that a theory of language, in any modern scientific sense of the word "theory," is probably not possible. Derrida has said something similar: "It is not certain that what we call language or speech acts can ever be exhaustively determined by an entirely objective science or theory" (1988, 118). As will be explained more fully below, this opinion is prompted by complications deriving from the unbounded nature of context.

While Derrida and Macksoud do not abandon the heritage of the Enlightenment, the particular laws that emerge from their views do move significantly beyond it. In this sense their approach is scientific but not strictly Enlightenment science and instead aligns more closely with the postmodern science of relativity and quantum physics. As with Macksoud's and Derrida's views of language, relativity theory and quantum mechanics problematize, while not eradicating, the notions of opposition, identity, causality, and context. This raises the difficulty of how to talk about, how to conceive of, structures that include and generate such essential possibilities. On one occasion, in the context of a discussion of deviancy, Derrida formulates the problem with the following question: "What must the structure called 'normal' or 'normative' be, what must the structure of the field where it inscribes itself be, for the deviant or the parasitical to be possible?" (1988, 126). In finding ways to talk about the structure of this "field," Derrida lays the groundwork for two additional laws, the basis for which may also be found in Macksoud's work. The first of these additional laws may be expressed as follows:

> The Second Law of Language (The Law of Iterability): Every repetition of a word is repetition *with a difference*; or iterability, as the repetition of words, always involves sameness and difference in an incalculable blend.

Derrida speaks of this law most directly in the 1977 *Glyph* essay "Limited Inc abc...":

> A standard act [speech act] depends...upon the possibility of being repeated, and thus potentially...of being mimed, feigned, cited, played, simulated,

parasited, etc., as the latter possibility depends upon the possibility said to be opposed to it. And both of them depend upon the structure of iterability which, once again, undermines the simplicity of the oppositions and alternative distinctions. It blurs the simplicity of the line dividing inside from outside, undermines the order of succession or of dependence among the terms, *prohibits*…the procedure of exclusion. Such is the *law* of iterability. (234)

Derrida immediately adds a qualification concerning how this "law" must be understood differently from the more traditional way of understanding "law":

Which does not amount to saying that this law has the simplicity of a logical or transcendental principle. One cannot even speak of it being fundamental or radical in the traditional philosophical sense. (234)

This departure from traditional philosophical sense derives from the origin of this law in *overdetermination* or a double determinacy Derrida refers to as "two-fold roots":

This is why I spoke of "two-fold roots" a while ago: two-fold roots cannot play the role of philosophical radicality. All problems arise from this non-simplicity which makes possible *and* limits at one and the same time. (234)

Derrida also describes this law of iterability in the course of a discussion of dehiscence:

Among other words, I have underlined *dehiscence*. As in the realm of botany, from which it draws its metaphorical value, this word marks emphatically that the divided opening, in the growth of a plant, is also what, in a positive sense, makes production, reproduction, development possible. Dehiscence (like iterability) limits what it makes possible, while rendering its rigor and purity impossible. What is at work here is something like a law of undecidable contamination, which has interested me for some time. (197)

This "law of undecidable contamination" corresponds to what Derrida calls "another general logic." Exceeding the Aristotelian logic of non-contradiction, this other logic describes the (non)logical space where a thing can both be itself and not be itself. How is such a paradox possible? Derrida responds in this way:

The concept of iterability…seems to me indispensable for beginning, at least, to account for all the difficulties that we meet in this field and in others…Doubtless the concept of iterability is not a concept like the others… That it might belong *without* belonging to the class of concepts of which it must render an accounting, to the theoretical space that it organizes in a (as I often say) "quasi"-transcendental manner, is doubtless a proposition that can appear paradoxical, even contradictory in the eyes of common sense or of a rigid classical logic. It is perhaps unthinkable in the logic of such good sense.

> It supposes that something happens by or to set theory: that a term might
> belong *without* belonging to a set. (1988, 127)

This alternative logic, with a paradox built into it, might appear to be a
purely theoretical construct that could not possibly relate to practical affairs. But
for good or bad, it is already describing in powerfully practical ways the world
of experience. This alternative logic resembles what is called "fuzzy logic" and
has succeeded in having enough practical application to launch a billion dol-
lar electronics and computer product industry by helping computers model the
blurred edge or oscillating categories relevant to the cybernetic recognition and
simulation of speech. Fuzzy logic augments computer bivalent coding with mul-
tivalent systems for more flexible and nuanced codings. Although Derrida would
probably not have looked favorably on the word "fuzzy" to describe his thinking, compare the following statement from the book *Fuzzy Thinking* to Derrida's
statement above:

> Every [traditional] philosophy or religion has a villain or devil it seeks to
> avoid or destroy. The villain of bivalence is the logical contradiction: A and
> not-A. In bivalent logic a contradiction implies everything. It allows you
> to prove and disprove any statement. Mathematicians scour their axioms to
> keep them from implying statements that contradict one another…[T]here
> is little tolerance in science for views that admit contradictions, that admit
> overlap between things and nothings. Fuzzy logic confronts this intolerance
> head on. Fuzziness begins where contradictions begin, where A and not-A
> holds *to any degree* [emphasis added]. (Kosko, 23)

As might be expected, fuzzy logic, like deconstruction, challenges classical
set theory, the relation between set and subset, container and thing contained, and
the boundary between the "inside" and the "outside." (cf. Kosko, 55-64)

The third of the laws that may be derived from the work of Derrida and
Macksoud concerns the boundary between text and context as the problem of the
"inside" and the "outside" and raises more directly the issue of relativity. This
law is found in Derrida's most notorious and most often misunderstood statement: *il n'y a pas de hors-texte*, (1974, 158) which is most famously translated as
"there is nothing outside the text." It may also be stated as follows:

> The Third Law of Language (The Law of Infinite Context): No point of
> view functions as "outside" a given text. Or, put differently, every attempt
> to maneuver into a transcendental vantage point on the text succeeds only
> in reforming the boundary (context) of the text, achieving only, as Derrida
> expresses it, "quasi-transcendence."

Contrary to how some have interpreted Derrida, this law does not mean that the book is all there is nor that the discursive world is the "real" world. It means, as Macksoud was cited as stating earlier, that nothing can be out of context—only in another context. At the risk of excessive citation, it is worth quoting Derrida once again because he has been so widely misunderstood on this point—as he expresses in exasperation in this passage:

> One of the definitions of what is called deconstruction would be the effort to take this limitless context into account, to pay the sharpest and broadest attention possible to context, and thus to an incessant movement of recontextualization. The phrase which for some has become a sort of slogan, in general so badly understood, of deconstruction ("there is nothing outside the text"…), means nothing else: there is nothing outside context…Once again (and this probably makes a thousand times I have had to repeat this, but when will it finally be heard, and why this resistance?): as I understand it…the text is not the book, it is not confined in a volume itself confined to the library. It does not suspend reference—to history, to the world, to reality, to being, and especially not to the other, since to say of history, of the world, of reality, that they always appear in an experience, hence in a movement of interpretation which contextualizes them according to a network of differences and hence of referral to the other, is surely to recall that alterity (difference) is irreducible. (1988, 136-137)

The text is always limitlessly extended into time, history, the world, and, thereby, into multiple unfolding contexts. No transcendent, outside, non-differential, non-deferred experience of the text is possible—other than the "quasi-transcendence" of which Derrida speaks that is in effect a recontextualization rather than a transcendence (traditionally understood). Quasi-transcendence reforms the perimeter of context while never escaping to a universal or absolute context.

It could perhaps be argued that an ultimate "stepping out" experience may be possible, as might be claimed in certain mystical experiences. Macksoud often abjured final pronouncements and exclusions by saying, "I have not had all the experiences there are to have." However, the kind of transcendence Derrida and Macksoud critique is not this kind of transcendence. Rather, they critique the kind of transcendence that would effectively authorize laying claim to an objective point of view capable of repetition *without* difference in communication and demonstration to others. For the world in which the possibility of communication exists, Derrida and Macksoud argue, no such transcendence seems possible, no such "outside" attainable. To attain it would at the same time end language and communication, because it would eliminate the circumstances, namely the repetition with a difference, through which they become both possible and necessary.

The Question of Relativity

The "incessant movement of recontextualization" Derrida and Macksoud address in their respective ways invokes a context for language-using in which there is no single anchor or foundation—like a polymorphous ellipse with not just two, but uncountable numbers of centers. More specifically, what does this shifting context suggest for understanding and interpreting language? Is language-using thoroughly relative? And if so, relative to what exactly?

The practice of deconstructive reading of texts assumes, to use a geological metaphor, that every text, posing as a uniform plate of meaning, has within it an undisclosed number of fault lines that, when discovered and pressed, produce tectonic shifts of the relation of parts within the text. These tectonic shifts then make possible the organization of the parts into new meanings corresponding to the new contextualizations.

Or, to use an optical metaphor, this shift resembles what takes place in "Stereogram" or "Magic-eye" images. These two-dimensional images, when looked at in a certain way, transform into a three-dimensional image. The image that was one becomes two; but the two oscillate back and forth, either one or the other but not both simultaneously—although, in a sense, each image "is there" simultaneously in what physicists refer to as "superposition." With each oscillation the "facts" of the image, its distinguishable parts and colors, are altered or organized into different "facts"; its unity or self-identity is divided, split into two images, two sets of facts. This duality of the image sets up an oscillation of an *undecidable* nature in that both images form or reform the "facts" to achieve a coherent impression.

It could be argued that this "Magic-eye" phenomenon is a special case and illustrates only that bizarre optical illusions can occur. But this would miss part of the analogy. Until the three dimensional image is seen—either through accident or coaching—*its possibility remains unknown.* When the possibility for such images is realized, many "naturally occurring" Magic-eye images may then get discovered. (The book *Super Stereogram* [1994], for example, contains several pages of "found stereograms" discovered in photographs that at first appeared to be simple two-dimensional pictures.) It cannot be known beforehand what alternative ways of seeing may open up. The problem may not be one of the rarity of the circumstances that permit such double vision, but a rarity of the flexibility for seeing in different ways.

Coaching and encouraging the flexibility for seeing in alternative ways is a part of the analogy corresponding to the role of the rhetorician in interpreting a text. Derrida argues (and Macksoud would agree) that the meaning of every text is undecidable; every text contains, as a necessary part of its ability to even function as a text, an undisclosed number of fault lines around which alternative understandings can be organized. Part of the job of the rhetorician consists of exposing the key fault lines that may open up new understandings. Readers of texts are not constrained to see or understand in particularly narrow ways. This means, as discussed earlier, that whatever the relationship may be between material structures (signifiers) and meanings (signifieds), it is not a linear causal relationship.

In cases of discussion, argument, persuasion, and communication, the boundary of a context is taken up, assumed, and shaped by the discourse of speakers; this boundary serves as a pragmatic limit or foundation for organizing the sense of what is said. But this foundation is not in any way objective or secure. It is tentative, provisional, experimental, in motion, and undecidably intersubjective. So, in any given occasion of discussion, conversation, or argument, certain meanings are working as provisionally foundational, but these meanings are not of special status and are not exempt from the trembling created by shifting fault lines. Every aspect of text and context always remains open to what Derrida calls solicitation, disturbance, destabilization.

Nevertheless, all the fault lines and corresponding trajectories or oscillations of a text cannot be made to tremble and shift at once—a constraint which preserves language from a certain kind of chaos. Such oscillations correspond, according to Derrida, to varying measures of *undecidability* between alternative understandings. Does this phenomenon of undecidability mean that one alternative is as good as another? May the meaning of a text be transformed with abandon or does something necessarily constrain the process? The answer, as might be guessed following the lead provided by Macksoud's previously mentioned postscript, is "probably yes."

Macksoud notes in the opening lines of *Other Illusions* that a distinction can and ought to be made between taste and judgment. Evaluation as a matter of *taste* occurs between competing alternatives of relatively equal value where the selection between them *will affect only oneself.* Evaluation as a matter of *judgment* arises from the same circumstance, but the choice from among the alternatives *will affect others besides oneself.* Macksoud points out that the behavior of someone who makes judgments as if they were matters of taste corresponds to that of a tyrant. Judgments require reasons, arguments, and persuasion where others are concerned; otherwise, the matter is no longer relevant to issues of language-using. And many people also require reasons for holding their own beliefs in the sense that they do not find it to be a cognitively consonant experience to cast a vote with the same casual fancy by which an after dinner dessert might be selected. But granting as much, what is to be done when confronted with, if Derrida is correct, "undecidable" alternatives? Does such a situation call for indecision, and, if so, how does any decision get made if undecidability haunts texts as doggedly as Derrida and Macksoud claim?

Undecidability, as Derrida uses the term, is not meant to suggest an impasse. It is intended instead to suggest that the material phenomena in question—symbols, signifiers, texts, etc.—do not and cannot, out of their own nature, enact a decision for the reader and interpreter of such phenomena. In other words, such phenomena do not present themselves in the manner of a calculation—however much that may appear to be the case on occasion. Here "undecidability" may perhaps be more clearly expressed as "incalculability" insofar as no decision can be algorithmically generated from the material data. The reasons for this circumstance, as already discussed, trace to the law of iterability. Furthermore, undecidability also implies that a choice presents itself to the interpreter between competing alternatives of relatively and apparently equal merit—as, analogously, in the case of Magic-eye images. In such cases, how do analysis and decision proceed? Certainly, in some such cases, a decision may not be required. But what of those cases where a decision seems necessary or desirable?

Macksoud and Derrida offer the answer that such situations call for judgment and judgment calls for reasons. The giving of reasons may be understood as argument, and, as already discussed, Macksoud maintains that argument is grounded in likeness and difference, the making of analogies and dysanalogies. And persuasive argument ultimately rests on persuading oneself or others what ought to serve as a relevant configuration of context. In other words, any possible decision in the face of "undecidability" must resort to or result from a strategic (in effect—whether intended or unintended) *recontextualization*. Recontextualizations, while perhaps displacing a particular undecidable oscillation in favor of one or the other pole, nevertheless open up new oscillations in ways that may or may not be immediately apparent.

The undecidability of texts necessitates judgment and surrenders itself only to recontextualization. Thus, decisions about the hierarchy, the superiority of one interpretation over another, are made on the basis of a *selected and argued* context. The responsibility of the rhetorician in selecting and exposing these contexts constitutes much of the substance of Macksoud's doctoral dissertation on the discovery of meanings in oral interpretation. Derrida's deconstruction makes the case that these contexts not be taken for granted. They are not entirely "given." They are provisional, arguable, debatable, and in most cases worth exploring (cf. Derrida, 1988, 136-137). Herein Macksoud and Derrida converge on a fourth and final law of language. This law, like the previous three laws, essentially repeats (with a difference) the same thing. And the force of the law is ironic in that it serves to show why there can be no law—in the sense of a reliably predictable science of meaning:

The Fourth Law of Language (The Law of Superimposed Contexts): Textual interpretation is always controlled by and relative to *contexts*. Being multiple, contexts overlap in, through, and beyond each other in "superposition." A corollary to this law asserts that interpretation (signification) is synonymous with contextualization—more precisely, *recontextualization* since everything is already necessarily contextualized—where recontextualization may be defined as the necessarily *partial* and thereby selective organization and mutual interpenetration of text/context. This corollary is essentially an elaboration of The First Law of Language with emphasis placed on the selectivity of context.

Here the word "partial" is borrowed from Macksoud as he explains that it must be understood in the dual sense, making reference to elements of quantity, as in "incomplete," as well as quality, as in "value weighted" or "hierarchical." Such partiality, however, opens the door to further consideration of relativity.

Newton conceived of motion as a function of context and in so doing moved physics in the direction of relativity. Einstein went further by showing that space and time not only do not provide an absolute context but instead necessarily give rise to multiple contexts, multiple spacetimes. With this pervasive relativity, the pure ideal of singularly valid measure becomes thoroughly "corrupted" through the lack of a fixed and universal point of reference. And the notion of "truth" is no exception to such complications—in physics as well as language.

One of the more shocking arguments Macksoud advances in *Other Illusions* reveals that, in one respect, he regards the truth-value of linguistic expressions to be on a par with matters of taste. Since he holds that all connections between the linguistic and the nonlinguistic are fundamentally analogy based, he expresses his critique of truth in the following way: "Analogies may be seen as possessing *equal truth-value*" [emphasis added] (1973, 76). With this assertion it would seem that Macksoud has gone too far.

Certainly, a case can be made for the view that the words of any text can be made to conform to any interpretation just as the facts of any situation can be made to conform to any theory. Anyone who has known an ardent believer in astrology knows this to be true. Every conceivable fact that can be marshaled to undermine and contradict the belief in astrology can be brought into conformity by some application of the theory, no matter how convoluted that application may appear to the non-believer. Even where there may be agreed on rules of evidence, it is difficult if not impossible to constrain the *application* of the rules by a further agreed on or transcendent set of rules. So long as a belief is rigidly held, there may be nothing that can assault it.

But in determining whether Macksoud has gone too far in his statement about truth-value, it may now be appropriate to select the most difficult of cases by which to test his claim. Some have argued that the Holocaust never occurred and that the apparent evidence can be explained away as, in one form or another, lies, deceptions, misunderstandings, or illusions. This revisionist view of the Holocaust stands in the starkest possible contrast to the views of survivors. How would Macksoud respond if he were asked: Do you regard the revisionists' and the survivors' explanations of the Holocaust as "analogies" possessing "equal" truth value? Is this an instance of undecidability?

Here it is necessary, abiding by the injunctions set forth already, to take care in understanding (provisionally and tentatively of course) the context of Macksoud's statement. If it is granted that the connections between the linguistic and the nonlinguistic are analogy based, then similarity rather than identity is the only guide. That being the case, it is fair to ask, along with Macksoud: "What is the criterion for similarity?...How much difference constitutes dissimilarity?" These questions lead Macksoud back to familiar ground:

> If nothing that I have called a matter of judgment before seemed a matter of judgment to you, I hope that you will assent to the proposition that the question of the presence or absence of similarity is a question of judgment, i.e., one for which we lack precise norms and measures. (1973, 77)

Macksoud argues that the mode of judgment corresponding to a transcendent or universal measurement or standard is a logician's slight of hand. Such transcendent judgment is understood in philosophical circles as the product of a transcendental subject. But the "transcendental subject" is not a *subject* at all; it is rather a *projection of objectivity*, having its foundation in a leap of imagination.

At bottom, Macksoud's arguments turn on what he calls the problem of the "disappearing judge." He is always preoccupied with making a case for the view that the judge cannot be eliminated from the judgment—as well as the deeper view and underlying value that the judge *ought not* to be eliminated from the judgment. As a consequence, Macksoud *recontextualizes*, or in Derridean terminology "displaces," rather than abandons the notion of truth; whatever other tests and ingredients may be required, the truth of linguistic expressions cannot be separated from the circumstance of being "*true by virtue of persuasion* which implies a judging mind" (1973, 79). Within this way of thinking it makes no sense to speak of an autonomous truth disconnected from the partiality of context.

But having displaced rather than abandoned the notion of truth, Macksoud's reference to "truth" in the statement that "analogies may be seen as possessing equal truth-value" must be understood as a reference to the traditional notion of truth as "correctness." And this much he makes clear a few paragraphs later:

Descriptions, definitions, or any application of language to a non-verbal entity—or even to another verbal one—are no longer regarded as differentially
correct, but rather as differentially *persuasive*...In short, language-using is
de-objectified and de-absolutized. (1973, 78)

Returning to the example of the Holocaust, it is now clear that Macksoud
will answer the question of the two views of the Holocaust by indicating that, in
different ways, they both address and account for *all the available facts* and in
this sense may be viewed as equally "correct." In other words, a theory or explanation has "truth-value" when it provides an account of all the available facts. But
both views need not be seen by particular judges as providing *equally convincing*
accounts. And the latter possibility generates an important shift in the meaning
and sense of "truth."

Those who lived through the Holocaust will not likely doubt their experience. Those who did not must rely on the material evidence and testimony of
others—evidence and testimony that pose the same problems of textuality and
iterability that Macksoud and Derrida have made apparent. Obviously, the evidence of such "texts" is not sufficient to *coerce* belief among any and all who encounter it, otherwise Holocaust revisionist thinking, to the extent it is genuinely
believed, *would not be possible*. Deconstruction *accounts* for the possibilities
of alternative interpretations (while not addressing all psychological factors that
may be involved in adherence to some possibilities of interpretation) but does not
thereby *authorize any and all interpretations*. Problems of textual interpretation
are not sufficient to make it impossible to form sober judgments. They are only
sufficient to recommend caution, care, and vigilance in examining the evidence
of any text.

Nevertheless, Macksoud's choice of the phrase "possessing equal truth-
value" may serve to mislead more than lead many readers—especially since the
word "truth" continues to have force in Macksoud's text by way of the recontextualization that aligns it with the criterion of *persuasiveness*. In the concluding
section, an alternative to Macksoud's choice of words will be offered. At this
point it is sufficient to say that for Macksoud the phrase "possessing equal truth-
value" does not reduce to or imply "possessing equal persuasiveness."

With the insistence on the "judging mind" behind every judgment, Macksoud would seem to reinstate a good measure of Descartes' *cogito* and along
with it the metaphysics of subjectivity postmodernists have expended considerable energy subverting. But Macksoud's "judge" is not another face of the Car-
tesian *cogito,* because it does not, in Kantian terminology, have at its foundation
any variation of a *transcendental* subject as a form of *pure* reason. Macksoud's
"judge" may be understood as a recontextualization of the subject in the form of

impure reason always embedded in particular temporal texts and contexts. This recontextualization of the subject matches Derrida's "resituating" of the subject. In an interview published in 1984, Richard Kearney asks Derrida for a prognosis of the subject in the aftermath of deconstruction:

> [Kearney] And what would you say to those critics who accuse you of annihilating the very idea of the human subject in your determination to dispense with all centralizing agencies of meaning, all 'centrisms'?

> [Derrida] They need not worry. I have never said that the subject should be dispensed with. Only that it should be deconstructed. To deconstruct the subject does not mean to deny its existence. There are subjects, 'operations' or 'effects' (*effets*) of subjectivity. This is an incontrovertible fact. To acknowledge this does not mean, however, that the subject is what it *says* it is. The subject is not some meta-linguistic substance or identity, some pure cogito of self-presence; it is always inscribed in language. My work does not, therefore, destroy the subject; it simply tries to resituate it. (Derrida, 1984, 125)

Derrida argues that the subject—more accurately, subjectivity—is an effect of *différance*. These effects also account for the phenomena referred to variously as "self," "consciousness," "person," and "individual." What is called the subject, then, is better understood as a site rather than origin of *différance*. And what is sometimes referred to as "the autonomy of the self" is better understood as an expression for the effects of difference through *différance*; that is, the self has effects of autonomy as *différance* has effects of difference. This view of subjectivity is entirely consistent with Derrida's maxim that "there is nothing outside the text." The subject (as effect) can no more get outside the text (and the effects of *différance*) than it can get outside context. The subject is always situated, inscribed within a context—a local, temporal, non-transcendental context—that includes itself as well as the text. When Macksoud argues that the judgment cannot be separated from judges or judging minds, he expresses the equivalent of Derrida's statement "there is nothing outside the text"—least of all the subject as "judge."

The possibility for something like judgment accounts for the possibility of persuasion. As already argued, the judgment called for in response to the undecidability of textual interpretation may be distinguished from calculation. Calculation may be likened to a form of coercion where conclusions follow with a singularly determinate, causally linked necessity. Persuasion, however, implies a flexibility of response belonging to the judgment required to assess multiple, overdetermined alternatives. Therefore, Macksoud's statement that "persuasion implies a judging mind" may be phrased in less egoic terms as: persuasion implies judgment—a judgment that never transpires automatically in the sense that a text never guarantees its own meaning.

Nor is the undecidable textual opening a space that is dominated or controlled by a subject whose freedom of choice is unconstrained. Terms such as "judgment" and "judging mind" serve to indicate the interval or divide between the certainty that a text can guarantee its meaning and the possibility that a text can mean anything. Persuasion is a phenomenon emerging from the necessity of this interval. As such it is a difficult matter to fully comprehend or definitively theorize. Regarding the judgments of which persons become persuaded, Macksoud confesses, "I know of no way to predict the ways in which these judgments may be achieved or influenced" (1973, 79). Nevertheless, what is called "reason" and the giving of reasons in justifications may be seen to belong to those operations humans attempt to impose as barricades against the tyranny of entirely willful and arbitrary judgments.

Macksoud goes on to acknowledge the possibility that the interval or divide that makes possible persuasion also opens the possibilities for willful interpretation: "If it is the case that inside every argument there is an analogy, it may be that inside every analogy is an act of sheer will" (1973, 79). This thought, as Macksoud is aware, brings the inevitable deconstructive queries, "Which will?", "Who's will?" If the phenomena referred to as "displacement," "recontextualization," "persuasion," and "judgment," record effects of selection, who or what selects? For the purposes of a certain convenience of discourse, the answer to this question may be "particular persons." But merely assigning a location, a personal name, to the effect called the "subject" may prove to be somewhat arbitrary and, thereby, uninformative. A more promising and perhaps more significant direction of response lies in rephrasing the question as follows: "What is the unique *quality* of the force (effects of differences) that may be perceived to move within or through particular persons as evident in their particular judgments?" Qualities of forces might be described as affirming, imposing, excluding, repressing, appropriating, etc. These qualities of forces may correspond to various economies of or attitudes toward oppositional tensions. While the force of will operating inside every analogy may be the "sheer will" of obstinacy, arrogance, or desperation, it may also be, among other subtle and endless variations, a probing will of explanation, interrogation, curiosity, care, and concern.

In summary, both Derrida and Macksoud abandon every notion of truth that functions as an absolute "outside." They separate truth from the automatic, the self-evident, the transcendent, and the purely disclosive and in doing so assert that it is better understood as a judgment—a judgment dependent on persuasiveness. Truth functions as the judgment of "judging minds" where each "judging mind" must not be too narrowly (or too broadly) construed as a transcendental subject accessing "pure reason."

Furthermore, with this recontextualization or displacement of the notion of truth, the opposition true/false, like space/time, no longer belongs to the order of opposition as discrete separation. The otherness of error, fiction, and falsehood always participates in the essence of truth as a consequence of the possibility of saying anything at all. To repeat Derrida's expression of this doubling of intention: "It [iterability] leaves us no choice but to mean (to say) something that is (already, always, also) other than what we mean (to say)" (1977, 200).

In the opposition of the relative/absolute, relativity wins out, but each term also submits to a displacement. Displaced relativity is not *vicious* and does not lead to narrow extremes of subjectivism or indeterminism. Its effects include possibilities for "quasi-transcendence" to which correspond contexts that provisionally transcend the particular, the individual, the subjective (e.g., Derrida, 1988, 136-137). The relativity of the multiplication of contexts retains a displaced sense of objectivity in the "quasi-" determinate effects occurring within the frames of oscillating alternatives, and, is in this respect, similar to Einstein's special relativity.

Granting as much, Derrida does not believe that deconstruction should be confused with relativism, since it does not imply the kind of radical relativism his detractors accuse it of—namely the relativism that asserts that one interpretation is as qualitatively good as another. In relation to human community, contexts and frames of reference endlessly overlap and are inseparable from each other even while retaining unique elements of difference, thereby guaranteeing that the persons responsible for these frames enter into modes of negotiation and evaluation with each other in the endless formation and deformation of community. The view of opposites that is central to all the discriminations laid out herein—that each side of the opposition is essential to the other—remains in force with regard to the tension between the relative and the absolute. To assert otherwise would be to pretend to understand too much about context.

What, after all, *is* context? Or to phrase the question in a way more consistent with the present argument: How should context be contextualized? Derrida has offered the following:

> The structure...supposes both that there are only contexts, that nothing exists outside context . . . but also that the limit of the frame or the border of the context always entails a clause of nonclosure. The outside penetrates and thus determines the inside. (1988, 152)

The problem of context repeats the problem of the sign which is the problem of every boundary. If meaning is relative to context, if context is bounded yet not bounded and thereby infinite, and if this context is split and doubled between the local and the general, between self and other, between "inside" and "outside," between part and whole, then the effect of relativity is also split. Emerging as what remains undeconstructible, the "other" or "otherness" serves not as absolute truth but as an absolute opening and thereby an *absolute limit* to truth and its accessibility. The question returns with a new force: Is every event of meaning finally relative or ultimately constrained by an absolute? The answer is, of course, "probably yes."

Conclusions

Macksoud's inquiry into language in *Other Illusions* ultimately delivers him to a position from which he is able to compose what he calls four "elementary propositions" toward a rhetorical view of language-using. This rhetorical view constitutes an orientation so inclusive in its fundamental outlook that Macksoud names it "radical strategism" by which he means the "strategy of excluding exclusions" (1973, 67). This approach is compatible with the way in which Derrida opposes the metaphysics of presence—a metaphysics he regards as a metaphysics of radical exclusion (for more on the metaphysics of presence as the metaphysics of exclusion and its alternatives, see Desilet 2002, Chapter Three). Macksoud's four elementary propositions are as follows:

1. The substance and forms of argument may be seen as analogy-based.

Since, as Macksoud hopes to have persuasively argued, no evidence precludes the possibility that all language-using rests on identities formed on the basis of contingent, context-bound judgments of similarity and difference, all argument, including the "arguments" of mere description, may be seen to rely on the construction of analogies.

2. Analogies may be seen as possessing equal truth-value.

This proposition and Macksoud's perhaps overly provocative use of the expression "truth-value" (by which he means to refer to the tradition of "truth" as objective fact accessible by all) may be productively amended to read as follows: Analogies may be seen as equally "correct" but also *equally exposed* to differentially constraining and constructive effects of contextualization. While these effects arise by default, context can also be seen to some extent as manipulable. Yet context always also exceeds such manipulation and, in that sense, always limits and thwarts control. The one who would manipulate context for personal gain remains always vulnerable to exposure rendered by more persuasive contextualizations. The adequacy of a particular analogy as a correspondence explanation can never be measured with certainty since a method of verification that will *guarantee* truthfulness does not exist anymore than does a form of expression that can *guarantee* communication—in each case for reasons having to do with the law of iterability. Persuasiveness, then, remains the ultimate ground for judgment. However, this consequence does not reduce to an expression of the form such as "Truth *is* that which one is persuaded is the case," but rather "That which, at any given time, one is persuaded is the case necessarily functions as the *provisional truth.*" This latter form becomes preferable by virtue of the belief that at no point in time do humans operate with anything other than provisional truth. The word "truth" then operates as shorthand for "provisional truth."

    3. Language-using may be seen as radically strategic.

    Language-using, or rhetoric, is *radically* strategic because the application of words, as in the act of naming, always requires an element of judgment in selective choice in contrast to the possibility of automatic or neutral computation.

    4. Rhetoric may be reformulated as an end in itself.

    In other words, rhetoric and communication need not be seen as fundamentally aimed at others or at persuasion of others. With this last reformulation, Macksoud initiates a shift in the standard of evaluation that appears to reduce rhetoric to the art of persuading oneself. But this overlooks the sense in which his approach is inclusive. Macksoud does not want to enshrine the individual while destroying communication. Rather, he wants to show that language-using is irrepressibly generative (of new meanings) and that as a consequence language is needlessly stripped of its character and potential when regarded as primarily and essentially a social tool or as constitutive of a social reality. Language may be at one and the same time, and to indeterminately equal extents, both social and anti-social—endlessly creating and tearing apart, connecting and disconnecting lines and networks of meaning. This view of rhetoric has the advantage of balance, of upholding value for both difference and sameness. Seeing language this way, understanding the limits of language, can only contribute to a healthy appreciation of the complexity of human interaction and to the importance of taking less for granted where self and others are concerned—all of which may add up to a measured tolerance that may promote a richer experience of life in general and social life in particular.

    Noteworthy for the present context, Macksoud began his career as a law school student and dropped out, because he saw that the legal profession was in the habit of asking more of language than language could deliver. Social order often demands of language that meanings be fixed and rigid—so that the law may simply apply itself. But language alone cannot do what social order would have it do. The need for judgment and, thereby, judges remains obvious.

Acknowledging the limits of language need not unravel the social fabric. Instead, it may make it stronger by showing where attention is most needed and by showing that effective writing of law and practice of law inevitably rest on quality of judgment. The fear remains, however, that truth made provisional is truth made human and partisan. Prosecutors, defenders, and judges—along with everyone else—may do their best to make words mean whatever may be needed for particular purposes. Nevertheless, this would appear to be a situation that language cannot be made to repair. Language, especially when pressed, will always return human community to the bottom line, to what it has required from the beginning, and to what words and the word of law can serve but never insure—trust in each other.

References:

Burke, Kenneth. 1966. *Language As Symbolic Action*. Berkeley: University of California Press.

Burke, Kenneth. 1984. *Permanence and Change*. 3rd Ed. Berkeley: University of California Press. (First published 1935).

Derrida, Jacques. 1974. *Of Grammatology*. Trans. Gayatri Chakravorty Spivak. Baltimore: Johns Hopkins University Press. (Orig. pub. 1967.)

Derrida, Jacques. 1977. Limited Inc abc...Glyph 2: *Johns Hopkins Textual Studies*. Trans. Samuel Weber. Baltimore: Johns Hopkins University Press, 162-254.

Derrida, Jacques. 1984. Deconstruction and the Other. *Dialogues with Contemporary Continental Thinkers: The Phenomenological Heritage*. Ed. Richard Kearney. Manchester University Press.

Derrida, Jacques. 1988. *Limited Inc*. Trans. Samuel Weber. Ed. Gerald Graff. Evanston: Northwestern University Press.

Desilet, Gregory. 1999. Physics and Language—Science and Rhetoric: Reviewing the Parallel Evolution of Theory on Motion and Meaning in the Aftermath of the Sokal Hoax. *The Quarterly Journal of Speech* 85:339-360.

Desilet, Gregory. 2002. *Cult of the Kill: Traditional Metaphysics of Rhetoric, Truth, and Violence in a Postmodern World*. Philadelphia: Random House Ventures, Xlibris Corporation.

Heidegger, Martin. 1977. Modern Science, Metaphysics, and Mathematics. Trans. W. B. Barton, Jr., and Vera Deutsch. *Martin Heidegger: Basic Writings*. Ed. David Farrell Krell. San Francisco: Harper Collins Publishers. (Orig. pub. 1962.)

Horibuchi, Seiji, Ed. 1994. *Super Stereogram*. San Francisco: Cadence Books.

Kosko, Bart. 1993. *Fuzzy Thinking: The New Science of Fuzzy Logic*. New York: Hyperion Press.

Macksoud, S. John. 1964. *The Literary Theories of Kenneth Burke and the Discovery of Meanings in Oral Interpretation*. PhD diss., University of California Los Angeles.

Macksoud, S. John. 1971. Phenomenology, Experience and Interpretation. *Philosophy and Rhetoric* 4:139-149.

Macksoud, S. John. 1973. *Other Illusions: Inquiries Toward a Rhetorical Theory*. Binghampton, NY: Privately Published.